AF248568

Meet Me at Carnegie Hall

Gwen Woodruff

i

Books by the same author:
    Dorset Forever   (published 1981)
    Return to Wessex   (published 1983)
    Come Away to England (published 1988)

First Edition

Library of Congress Catalog Card Number 92-93256

Printed in U.S.A.

Font — Times Roman, 12 pt.

Published by Woodruff Publishing Co.
4153 Kennesaw Drive
Birmingham, Alabama 35213 USA

ISBN 0-9616165-3-9

Meet Me
at
Carnegie Hall

*Sketches and designs
by the author*

Birmingham, Alabama
1992

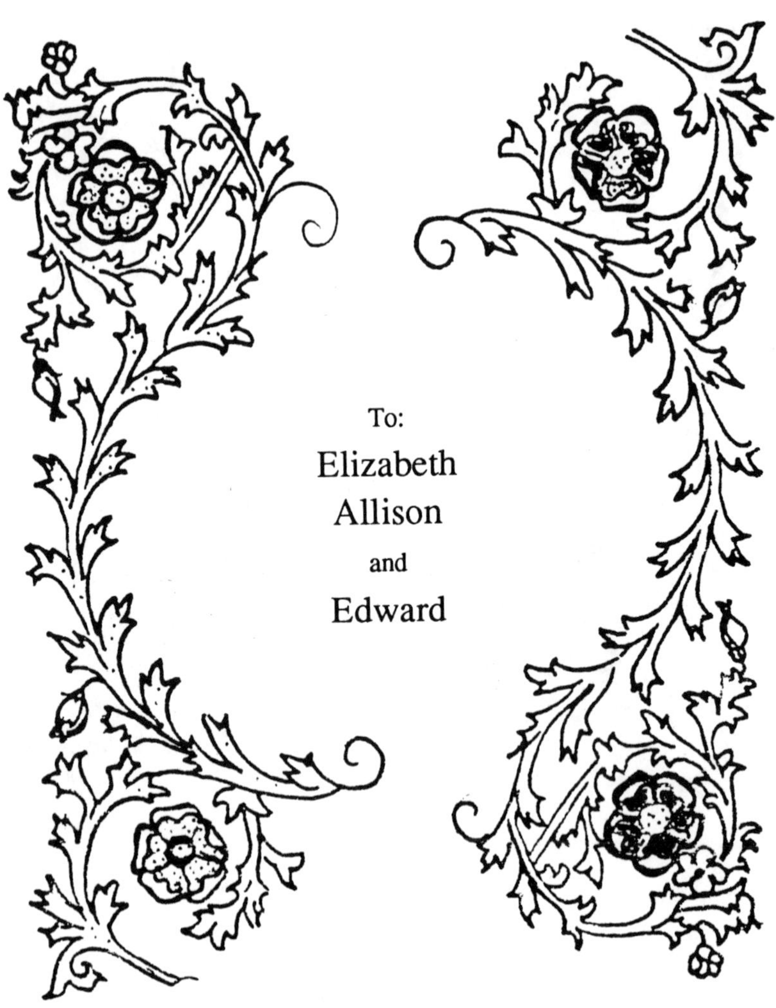

To:

Elizabeth

Allison

and

Edward

MEET ME AT CARNEGIE HALL

Gwen Woodruff

Synopsis

A tragic and powerful moving story laid in the exquisite background of Western European scenery. It is a sad tale of a pure woman undaunted by human, hopeless situations . . . and her ability to rise above them.

There is comedy and pathos; the author has the ability to turn tears to laughter in the turn of a page.

Re-acquaint yourself with history and reshaping of the world from the mid-nineteenth to the mid-twentieth century.

This story is based mostly on European history with the fictional character, Rose, weaving in and out of a series of chronicles that make up the hundred year period from 1844 to 1944; the most dramatic era since civilization began. It can be summarized by the following list of actual persons in the narrative.

William the Conqueror	1066
Uncle Jessie (the sweater man)	1924
Eekie	1924
Wendy (the author)	1924
Miss Force	1900's
William Wyatt Bibb - 1st governor of Alabama Territory	
William Rufus King	1821
Edwin Hughes - New York Concertist and Teacher	
Frédéric Chopin	1809-1849
J. S. Bach	1685-1750
John Henry Newman	
Richard Wagner	1813-1883
Cosima Wagner	
George du Maurier	
Gerald du Maurier	
Daphne du Maurier	1903-1989
Queen Victoria	
Lord Palmerston	
Walter C. MacFarren	1826-1906
Bismarck	

Franz Josef (Austria)
Carl Tausig   1841-1871
Franz Liszt   1801-1886
King Frederick William III
Sir Arthur Sullivan   1842-1900
Napoleon III
Honoré Daumier
King Ludwig II (Dream King)
Oskar Von Miller (Founder of
   Deutsch Museum)
King William I of Prussia (Emperor
   of Germany 1871-1888)
Emperor William II ("Kaiser Bill"
   1888-1918)
Thomas Hardy (author)
Lord Courtenay of Powderham Castle, UK
Claude Debussy   1862-1918
Van Gough
Titanic
Lusitania

Fiction, Rose Edleigh and family

MEET ME AT CARNEGIE HALL

PROLOGUE

1920... Growing up in a Small Southern City...

Everyone said the old lady that lived next door was quite old... ancient, in fact. That Saturday morning the town looked deserted; all were at the Live Oak Cemetery paying their respects,... some, being it was the first of the hot season, possibly wanting an occasion to show off their new summer finery in the small community, where there were so few opportunities for doing so.

We youngsters thought Miss Edleigh had lived about a thousand years 'cause she was always telling us about the Frenchman who had been "transfused" with English blood and came to England to take the throne away from Harold, who argued that it had been promised to *him* by the gentle King Edward the Confessor. William, a cousin of the Confessor, swore it was *himself* that it was to go to. But nothing was put in writing... so a big fight started, I mean like a war. William won by shooting an arrow upward, and while Harold was surveying the sky, it fell right smack in his eye. The

Frenchman across the Channel became King William the Conqueror. Miss Edleigh had seen the very spot where it happened -- so we knew it was true. Oh, the many things she told us; she always served up her adventures with lemonade and gingersnaps. There was an old brute of a king that had six wives -- none of them pleased him 'cept the one who died on account of **he** wanted a son so bad! And she (Miss Rose) said she cried when she saw the block where he chopped so many heads off. I learned also what "he met his Waterloo" meant... 'cause she'd been there where Napoleon met **his**. Gosh, she must 'ave been old! But what did she have to go and die for!

*Edward
the Confessor*

Well, everybody is at the Resting Place this morning and I don't know what else to do... I'm not going up that fig tree again 'cause last time I was stung by a bumble bee that I mistook for a Junebug. We always kept one on a string -- a Junebug, I mean -- and walked him around like he was a kite or helium balloon. But I ain't ever going to tie strings on those things again.

My best pal across the street has gone to Bond, Mississippi, where she spent every summer with her Aunty Wiggings. Heck, what was the use of school being out if there's nothing to do. For a while I gathered flowers -- little wild ones -- and dug a hole deep enough to put a bowl in, and lined it with ferns. I then laid the frail little posies side by side in the declivity. In the garage was a half broken windowpane that I washed and placed over the flowers, spreading the scooped-out dirt over the edges of the glass. Now I had a peep-show. I would charge everybody who passed by a penny to peep. Here came Brooks, our postman. "Well, Miss, I've got one cent left." I thought surely someone else would show -- but they didn't. I must have fallen asleep under the big magnolia 'cause next thing I knew Mama was nudging me to get up.

"It was a wonderful funeral... everybody is going to miss that old lady. You should have seen Uncle Jessie -- all dressed in his Sunday finery. There was some sort of mystery to her life before she came here. I wonder what it was!"

But nobody was going to miss her like me. She'd lived next door all my life and she'd always be there to me!

"This just came for you, Wendy. Miss Rose Edleigh told her lawyer that it was for the little girl next door," said Mama, answering the front knocker.

"Oh..h.h..," my voice trailing off in disappointment; "a tablet!" and I put it in my bottom drawer. It was a sorry summer. The big depression was on -- whatever that meant; Miss Edleigh would've explained it. She would have told me why they said men were jumping off tall buildings in Birmingham and other big cities, and why folks didn't have much money... and stuff like that. Shux, why did she have to go and die that way... and stop making gingerbread!

Somehow summer passed. I had become eleven. All the older kids said I was 'in for it' -- I was getting Miss Force for homeroom and history. I found out what they meant soon enough. Sixth grade was hard. When the class got noisy she had a habit of slamming her palms together and screaming "freeze". Whoever moved after that warning -- woe to him! So we opened the Alabama History text... and first off, she slipped her glasses on and looked straight at me. "Wendy, who was the first governor appointed to the Alabama Territory? Stand up, please." I stood... how did I know that William White, sitting at the desk behind me, had already attached a provocative slip of paper on my skirt. Everybody snickered and I found out why and blurted out, "William,... William!" and Miss Force said, "Yes, yes dear, William *who*?" And my embarrassment was terrible... "William White" --

"Go on, what was his last name?"

"Err-a -- I can't think, teacher."

"Well, you got part of it right. It was William Wyatt Bibb. I'll give you some credit on that."

But I knew that wasn't honest -- I hadn't the faintest idea of the answer to her question -- and I felt guilty. When I reached home I was in no mood for communication with anyone. I went to my room and pulling out the bottom drawer, gathered the tattered old manuscript that Miss Edleigh had left me. I missed her so! Ordinarily, I'd be over there telling her my troubles -- and she'd know exactly what to do to soothe my feelings. Now, what on earth would she have told me! She'd probably say, "There, there, little pal, no harm done... you *did* learn something, didn't you? Let's get out that old history book and see who made Mr. W. W. Bibb the first governor." And then she would have told me the whole thing and made it sound like an exciting story: -- and I'd hate when the phone would ring and we'd be interrupted.

I clutched the brown paper bag to my heart... but I couldn't open it yet... not so soon. It still had a faint smell of Cape jasmine about it. Jeepers! It's after four o'clock and I haven't done my piano yet. Mama will kill me when she gets home from P.T.A. -- Oh, me, and she will have heard about my acting a dunce in history today. She always asks the teacher, "How is Wendy doing?"

"Well, Wendy could do much better than she does... she's a dreamer. She could go far with the proper incentive. Her music ability exceeds her age by many years; but you know she has to go through the discipline of required academic subjects regardless of her talent in other pursuits."

Yep, I caught it when Mama came in the front door. "No more music, Missie, until you bring up the history grade!"... And I almost had the Mozart memorized! Needless to say 'history' improved--- but I didn't like it any better. What I needed was Miss Edleigh, she'd make it good and interesting.

That night I had a strange dream. It was real as life. My old friend's house was to be sold. When I saw the new owners pull up in their fancy new T model Ford car, I ran out and entered the rear window that was always opened to air things -- and put the back of a chair under the front door knob. They pushed and pushed and were so puzzled over it that they got back in their car and drove away. Making my retreat the same way I entered, I knocked over a small chest -- its contents scattered to the floor: hundreds of sheets of paper, and on top was a mildewed copy of my beloved "Mozart." I awakened just after the window slipped from its catch and penned me inside.

I sat up in my bed -- the moon was full. Not bothering to dress, I slipped outdoors, parted the hedge and crept to the house -- the sash was not locked so I retraced the steps of my dream. A scrap of paper stuck out of the chest drawer and I opened it and found this in Miss Edleigh's cramped and rigid writing: "To Wendy from Miss Rose... I know you will 'make it' someday." It was a book entitled *Great Pianist on Piano Playing*, by James Cooke.

I felt the first tears I had ever shed for any reason other than my own wounds -- and vowed on the spot: "I *will* make it, too!"

The next day I used study hall to do my math; I listened in class to every word the teacher said, and hurried home... not even going the long way to avoid a house where they said "chinks" lived who snatched little girls. I grabbed a glass of milk and lit in on Alabama History. The book opened up to a part that I was supposed to have already studied, but I started reading... and it told about the Battle of Burnt Corn in 1813. Several hundred Indians had gone down to Pensacola for guns and ammunition (I knew where that was; I'd spent enough long summers there and in Burnt Corn with Grandma.) It was bloody alright, and the 'Red Sticks' got the best of the deal. War was on then, next was the Fort Mims Massacre. The Red Men pillaged the countryside far and wide, burning houses and collecting white scalps and doing whatever bad they could do. Gosh, this was getting good!... better'n a picture show. The most exciting thing to happen in the Creek War was about a scouting party that spotted a big canoe floating down the Alabama River with eleven Creek warriors. Three Americans rowed out in a small canoe with Caesar, an Indian Negro, at the oars. A few guns were fired and Caesar pulled over to the Indian craft. The Negro held the two boats together while the three white men clubbed the Indians 'til they were dead and then threw them in the river.

By the time I finished the 'Creeks and Chickasaws' I was up to 1837. Well, history isn't so bad, but I had spent two of the afternoon's precious hours. Now it was time to set the table for supper. After drying the dishes I still had English to do -- but I liked that. Mama had locked the piano! I guess she really meant 'no more music until grades came up'. Things got better by degrees, but I pined for my forbidden ivories. I exercised my fingers... going through all the scales and arpeggios on the table top 'til the drumming rhythm must have driven everyone crazy. I hoped so! Finally, report card day... There! History, C+. Glory be! Mama produced the magic keys and unlocked the piano lid.

"By the way, Wendy, what was in that brown bag that the lawyer sent you?"

"I don't really know, but you can look if you like."

She did, and started reading the old manuscript. I slipped out the door unnoticed. By now the new family next door had settled in. They had a twelve year old son and a girl of ten. Anxious to play the 'stupid mausoleum' game on them, I wooed them off to the near-by cemetery on the street behind our houses. On the main avenue that ran through the graveyard there was a magnificent square marble tomb that housed the remains of William Rufus King, who not only founded Selma, where we lived, but had been elected vice-president of the United States of America. That was what made me most proud of my hometown!

I led the two 'usurpers' (I never was going to accept these two for friends) through the big wrought-iron gates, past the Indian Princess' grave and all the tall monuments -- obelisks, I think they call them -- and there it was. The great black door was additionally secured with spider webs that almost became a piece of fabric. Lighting the candle I'd brought, I set it up securely. My companions said, "Come on, get it over with." I closed my eyes and lisped some mumbo-jumbo in ghostly solemnity, then told them we were going to commune with the dead. "Ah, you can't do that," said Wilbur........ "Sh, sh, now knock on the door three times and say, 'William Rufus, what are you doing in there' and encircle the tomb three more times asking the same question." On the third go round, he hesitantly inquired: "William Rufus King, what are you doing in there?" Complete silence followed -- and he waited with his ear to the keyhole.

"Ah, you liar! He said nothing at all...."

"There, see... you got your answer. He was doing nothing at all!"

Disgusted, the brother and sister ran out of the cemetery. I loitered on, passed lots of family plots enclosed with iron grill-work and came to the simple stone slab of Miss Edleigh's. On the head marker it had some words cut in the marble that said,

I rest not here, but have gone to
Be home with my dear Creator and His Son,
Who, in obedience to His Father, allowed the
World to crucify Him so that all who believed in
His Love would join Them in the days to follow our
Allotted time.

Then I remembered her stories about Pilate and the Pharisees and the Scribes. She would close them by singing, "Were You There When They Crucified My Lord?" I even thought I could smell her gingerbread for a fleeting moment.

Boy, it was getting dark -- I better beat it home... Too late. Sundown had caught me day-dreaming and I was locked up in the place of the dead for the night. By now Mama must be frantic. So I did an awful thing. There was a sunken grave close to me and the slab was broken in two pieces. By my tugging and twisting to the right and to the left, it finally came to a halt against the five-foot-tall wall. When I got one foot up I thought to hoist myself the rest of the way over, but the stone rocked over and I landed in the depressed earth on the sunken grave. My ankle was shooting pains up my leg.

Meantime, the investigation at home had started. The kids next door shrugged their shoulders and said they'd left me in the cemetery. Mr. Pheiffer, the super-intendent, got his keys and unlocked the gates -- he just lived across the street. Well, I was found in a state of misery. The Doc said I'd have to stay off that foot.

After the relief of finding me safe -- then she started the lecture. In the middle of the harangue that I knew was going to go on forever, I interrupted her with what I was really worrying about. "Mama, where do folks go when they die?" She looked stunned, "Well, Wendy, when somebody's led a good life and obeyed the Ten Commandments... and gone to church, they will be taken to Heaven."

I wasn't satisfied with that..., "No, Mama, it's something else more than that -- or I guess *less*! Miss Edleigh never went to any churches... but there was sumpin' in her eyes that always misted up when she talked about the Crufixation... I mean Crucifixion. When she told us kids Bible stories, she said 'em just like she'd been there, and I know she wasn't that old... 'cause her tombstone said, 'born 1844 -- died 1920.' Must be 'cause she felt them so real! Like when Jesus hung on that dern cross..."

"Wendy! Hush your mouth, don't you ever say a word like that again."

"Well, that thing they nailed Him to... and He just let 'em do it, looking down with love in His eyes at the people. Then He asked God to forgive them."

"I suppose, then, you better start a little forgiving, yourself. The children next door in the Poderfoy house can't help it because they live there -- in fact, their behavior is far better than yours. Isn't it time you made a truce with them?"

That ended our discussion for the day. Guess I'd have to figure out all that theology myself. That night I rushed through my English essay and crept into the parlour for the heavy leather-covered Testament with the gold-edged pages. The book flopped open at Matthew -- oh, he was a publican who collected taxes for

the Roman government, and hated by the good Jews...
it read, "But if ye forgive men their trespasses, your
heavenly Father will also forgive you." -- But Wilbur
wasn't really trespassing by moving into 'her' house.
This has to mean something else. So I started reading
more and more in the Book. I figured that 'trespassing'
meant 'sin'. As days went by this 'secret reading' became more irresistible -- and now it was like a passion
with me. I wasn't feeling that Miss Edleigh was so far
away.

Next month, in December, I was going to join the
church, as most of us kids did on reaching twelve; also
I was playing on a special music program at Mr. Meek's
studio. My mother was glad that only one dress would
do for both occasions. It was white... kinda' off-white
'cause she was making it from one of her old ones. But
it was real pretty with a big rose-colored sash that tied
in the back. "Can I tie my hair on the top like the lady
in the picture with a pink bow?"

"Not for church, but for the recital."

I never worked so hard -- Mama worked hard,
too, on my dress. There just weren't hours in the day
to get in all the practice I wanted on the piano. My
teacher was a good one, having been a student of
Edwin Hughes in New York City. She hammered into
me constantly about the C scale. "Get that thumb under! Curve your fingers, loose wrists! Each note like a
shiny pearl in a string -- bright and smooth. The C
scale is the hardest one of all because it's the only one
without a black key. Wendy, there are eighty-eight
notes on the board, you have only five fingers on each
hand; the only way to cover the area is to make the
thumb play about eight times better than the fingers.
Your scales must sparkle with the beauty of splendid

gems -- you'll not find them in shallow waters. Dig deep, my girl."

Wilbur, next door, was forgotten for the time being. I was going to show Mama and Papa that they were not wasting money on piano lessons, so his and my animosity was not exercised toward each other for a while.

Last Sunday, I stood at the altar rail and joined the church. I looked the minister in the eye when he asked those serious questions and I said, "I do solemnly --" -- it was like getting married, sorta. It actually felt as if I had acquired a halo.

The night came for the musical. The big fat woman sang loud and high, sometimes sounding like Mrs. Rossly at Grandpa's farm calling the hogs. When she finished, I was on next to play the last movement of the Mozart Sonata called "Alla Turca" -- or "Turkish March." The seat was too low... it had to be screwed up on the sides to raise it. So I reached for the gadget and kept turning and turning... it surely needed oiling. Now I was at the right level, but I felt a draft and as I moved my position it was as though I was caught... or being tugged at. The little wheel of the mechanism had chewed into my skirt and wound it up to my thighs. The program leader saw my predicament and relieved the situation. Everybody clapped loudly, and I (the 'ham' I was) took a deep exaggerated bow. Smoothing out my dress and announcing, "So much for the floor show," I sat back down on that der- (woops) chewing machine, paused a moment and raised my arms. I never played with as much vigor and ease! The audience stood clapping when I finished the last note. Then I *really* did some bowing and ran off stage.

My mother and father were beaming; the piano

teacher was strutting and I was sleepy! The next day
was Sunday; my older brother would drive Eekie (that's
what I called my best friend) and me to Sunday school.
Eekie and I were almost like twins, there was only one
day between our birthdays, and our mothers were both
members of the Eastern Star... 'cause our fathers were
Masons. She was the smart one; even though Mama
set her up as an academic model, it didn't hurt our
friendship -- for I knew I could do some things better
than she could. Whenever the Eastern Star ladies met
at night, I was permitted to sleep over at her house.
But back at the church that particular day... guess I was
feeling a bit impish, what with the piano performance
over. Something got into me. That big fat soprano was
sitting in the pew in front of us! My forehead 'itched
and I pushed back my invisible halo.' The offering
envelopes were in the rack at arm's distance. I took
one... and when we got up to sing "Shall We Gather At
The River," I licked the pasted flap and laid it sticky-
side-up just in time for the congregation to be seated.
"Boy, wait 'til the 'blackdress' stands up to say the
Apostles Creed. Did it *work*! Eekie and I stifled our
giggling -- the whole row of seats vibrated with our
silent quivering bodies. Mama at the other end of the
curved pew looked over at where we sat. Her glance
said, "I'll see you when we get home, my girl!"

Needless to say, we did get home. I was allowed
to eat dinner in my room, no dessert. Then I thought
of what William White had done to me... that was *no*
comparison to the deed I committed in God's house! --
"I am so sorry, God, please forgive me; I'll never let the
devil sway me again... but please don't always make me
have to be behind the fat lady. Amen."

(I felt terrible when Mama said Mrs. Fatzwald

had a heart attack and died the next week.) But to the present: with the rest of the day spent in my 'boudoir'... what to do! As I stood by my window, I saw my old friend 'Uncle Jessie' approaching. He had always done chores for Miss Edleigh. Catching his attention, I motioned him over to my window. "Ask Mama if you can see me,... please, Uncle Jess; I've got so much to ask you."

Jessie Adam was a coal-black Negro and as kind and honest as a preacher... maybe more. The man wanted to get some work to do, as his family was in bad shape, money-wise. Miss Edleigh had seen to it that his daughter went to Paine University in the town where we lived. His employer's death had devastated him as he not only lost a friend but lots of benefits as well. Mama told the new people in the Poderfoy house about what good work he did, and his honesty, so they hired him. He was very happy with the jobs they wanted done. So he went round back and said, "Miss Dolly, can I see Wendy a minute?" I was called into the kitchen where Uncle Jess was drinking a cup of coffee Mama'd fixed him.

"Now, Miss Wendy, what be on your mind? Are you being nice to the new-comers next door?"

After a long sip from his cup, he looked deep into my eyes. There were tears in his... "We both miss her so much, don't we, lamb-chile."

And he told me how she was better off -- how badly she suffered from her paralyzed arm, and for the loved ones she'd lost. "In Europe, she had been a great piano player, but she never told nobody but me. But, chile, you was sech a blessing to that old lady -- she would talk to me about you... how much you were like herself when she was a little one. I was at her side when she died and the last thing she said was for me to look after the little girl next door. Why you think I want to work for those folks in her house so bad!

"Let me tell you something that you wouldn't know: when you wuz littler -- maybe 'fore you'se born -- there wuz a shabby ole man that went about town doin' odd jobs: trimming trees, cleaning chimneys, raking leaves and sech. He wuz an ugly ole fellow, he had nothing to make him smile... and nobody cared if he didn't! The little children would see him a'coming down the street with his coil of ropes around his shoulder and his axe a'swinging in his hand, and they'd call all they's friends and start jeering: 'Here comes the sweater man -- mean old sweater man. Run for your lives as fast as you can!'

"So one day, I started running toward 'em swinging my axe and they flew swifter than the wind to their mamas saying I wuz gone' kill 'em. Well, de front door opened in that house next to you and a white lady called out to me, 'Are you looking for some work to do? I have a tree limb that I want removed... could you handle it for me?'

"I went round to the back door and told her I would. She gave me a cup of coffee and a little cake and said to knock on the window when I wuz through and she'd pay me. When I finished cutting, I started stacking up all the limbs to be hauled away. Then I rapped her window.

'You do good work. I have many things to be done to the yard, can you come back next Thursday?' and she counted out the money in my hand, 'and here's fifty cents extra for the neat way you cleared the place.'

"The next week I came back to her house, and she told me to come in for some coffee. Then she said,

'Jessie, why do the children taunt you so?' And I answered, 'cause my heart's so black... it ain't just my skin! You know, Miss, you is the only one that's ever been good to me... and I's been full of anger, I guess. I don't remember having a mama or papa... jes been on the streets doing work for food.'

"She said, 'Jessie, I am Rose Edleigh, and I want to help you. We start out this way. You're not going to work today. Can you read? -- no? I will teach you.'

"She brought out a big book and opened it up and read: 'God so loved the world, that He gave His only begotten Son, that whosoever believeth in Him should not perish, but have everlasting life.' She made me memorize that 'fore I left her house, and she put it in print for me to look at when I got home. (Home was in the back of a farmer's barn.)

"I was paid for full work time and she gived me extra pay to buy a hat. All week long I kept saying that verse over and over. I traced the letters she made 'til they looked almost like I'd been to school. It made me feel so glad all over that the next Thursday I whistled a tune when I 'proached her house and I didn't hear any chillen yelling at me -- in fact, they'd lost their interest."

I put my finger up to his face and caught a tear. "Uncle Jessie, I try to be good, but it seems I've got an imp inside of me that makes me do things I ought not to. I don't tell lies or really hurt anybody, but I don't like people who pretend, and I get 'even' with them... and I know I'm not supposed to. I thought when I joined the church everything was going to be easy."

"Oh, me, no. That's when ole Satan got his busiest -- he didn't like it when you stood up for God 'fore de congregation. You'll just have to pray more about it. Let's do it now 'fore I leave: 'God, in heaven, look down on this chile of Yours. She's goin' through some hard times -- don't let de devil get near her. And tell Miss Edleigh we still love her. Amen.'"

The old man left and I went back to my room with lots of resolves. Miss Edleigh said nobody could keep the Ten Commandments -- they were just a mirror to show how far short we fall from being holy. So that's why Jesus had to be the sacrifice for our sins. But we had to believe that and accept it with all our heart. I knelt by my bed and told God that this time I meant it -- no more pranks. "And I'll show other folks that I love You. Amen."

School got better in lots of ways -- and before I knew it, it was May; one more month to go. I was now into Chopin... "The Minute Waltz." At my next lesson, my piano teacher introduced me to her visiting friend, who was well known in the music world. He listened to my lesson and seemed deeply interested in my performance. He placed his hand on my head and said, "Little lady, you have an artist in you. Cultivate your individuality and avoid imitation. You'll be great some day."

Wow, really! I walked home in an excitement I'd never felt -- my feet hardly touching the ground -- just sorta' floating along. Thoughts came to me about the brown sack in the bottom drawer, and entering the house I headed straight for it.

I began reading the story of Miss Edleigh's life.

Rose's Story.

CHAPTER 1

England ... 1844. To Wendy.

In Hampstead Heath, North London, they gathered around the little crib, all agreeing she wouldn't survive the night. It was a difficult delivery that had cost the mother's life. The wet-nurse and Nanny promised the father that baby *would*! And she did. I was that child. Nanny was a youngish middle-aged woman with a passion for children and music. Father was away so much of the time that, as I outgrew my baby days, I wondered who the strange man was down in the parlour. Nanny explained he was an important man and had to travel to lots of far away places -- India, Africa and America.

Soon I started noticing the world I lived in with it's lovely sounds and colorful birds, and how the water in the pond splashed when I threw a pebble in. I must have been three. For a long time, I had sought the beautiful piano, hitting one note after another imitating Nanny's songs that had lulled me to sleep. She would seat me at the keyboard and say, "Rose, this is C. Look, there are two black keys then three black ones -- then two and then three all the way from one end to the other. Now C is the white one on the left side next to the two black ones." I was delighted to see how many C's there were. By now I knew my ABC's and could count to twenty. She placed my index finger on C and told me to play "God Save The King." I listened to her voice go up and down and followed it on the keys... and greatly overjoyed at my accomplishment cried out, "I will tell Papa when he comes!" She said, "No, you will *play* it for him."

The next day she put my left hand on the piano with my little finger, my 'pinky', on the C below middle C, and pressed down the third finger and thumb (my hands were unusually large and "sorta' ugly," I over-heard the housekeeper tell my nurse). They fell just on the correct notes. "That's a C chord. Now see if you can put it with what your right hand played yesterday." I obeyed, "Oh, Nanny, I can play piano!"

When Mr. Edleigh returned from his long trip Nanny greeted him with, "Sir, you have a musician." My father gathered me in his arms and swung me high in the air -- I scrambled down to show him what I'd learned. He didn't get a chance to remove his scarf and topper.

"Nanny, will you see if you can find a teacher for one so young?" "No, Sir, I will teach her myself."

So everyday we took thirty minutes before lunch to explore the wonderful music, and the relationship of the printed note to the sounded one on the piano. On my fourth birthday I went to my first concert with Papa. Nanny had picked a beautiful pink dress with lots of ruffles and a sash of deep rose tied in the back. Life ran on this way for another year and I became five years old. Papa was delighted -- it seemed he stayed at home more these days.

The great Chopin was giving a concert in London -- one of his occasional ones, for his health was very poor. It was early in the year of 1849 -- just before he died after his return to Paris. The famous musician shook hands with me when my father said I was to be a concert pianist some day. I never forgot that music he played -- nothing was ever so beautiful. Nanny told me that Chopin was born in Poland, but his father was from France and his mother was a Pole.

"Oh, you mean she was a bean pole!" laughed Rose. "No, silly, she was a Polish lady from Poland." Parts of Poland were seized by Austria, Russia and Prussia; they wanted to destroy Poland. All of Chopin's boyhood was fraught with sorrow over his homeland, and most of his compositions reflect that sadness.

"He gave his first public recital at the age of twenty in Vienna. But I'll bet you will give yours before you're that old. Chopin practiced nothing but Bach while preparing for his appearances. Soon we are going to start on Johann Sebastian Bach's works. He was the father of Contrapuntal music, or, as it's sometimes called, 'Counterpoint.' When a group of voices sing a 'round' -- like when we did 'Row, row, row your boat gently down the stream,' the first singers continue 'merrily, merrily, merrily, merrily life is but a dream' --

but the second singers start in on the first line -- and it goes on and on.   That's called a two-part invention. We'll get started on Mr. Bach next week."

I became six years old and Nanny let me have a birthday party. One of the guests didn't like another girl and pushed her in the pond. My, my, what an upset!   The party broke up before refreshments got served. But I enjoyed opening my gifts after they left -- and there'd be plenty of cupcakes and goodies to last a long time!

My father got to thinking about my schooling; he somehow didn't think my Nanny was capable of that -- so a governess was decided on. There was interview after interview before Papa picked Miss Plimpsted. She would live at our house, which didn't sit well with Cook. And after a few days there was a quarreling in the kitchen. Cook said *she* was boss of the culinary quarters and Miss Plimpsted had better quit sending special notes and requests for some delicacies that never had been served in that household... and if they *were*, they'd be prepared by a new chef! Well, she meant it, 'cause three days later there was a new woman doing our meals. Things dragged on -- Nanny still taught me my piano lessons. But the classroom that had been set up in my old nursery wasn't to my liking. The governess had me reading baby stories that made me puke! And heck, I'd been doing sums for ages with Nanny. Nothing was going right. When Papa arrived from Hong Kong this time he was greeted with harangue and bickering -- bedlam in general. Miss Plimpsted said either she'd leave or Nanny would have to go. But Nanny, overhearing it all, went upstairs and packed her belongings and left silently by the back door. She was trying to spare Mr. Edleigh the worry.

Days passed and I didn't touch the piano -- my heart was broken. And on one certain night I slipped away from the house. I thought I knew where Nanny lived, but I didn't realize how big a city -- even a suburb like Hampstead -- could be. The rains came, first little scattered drops, then the skies opened up. After walking, walking and walking I came to something like a conduit, a big drainage pipe -- I was soaked, so I climbed inside to rest. Needless to say the household had gone hysterical when they discovered a six-year old not occupying her bed the next morning. The police were called in -- search parties sent out everywhere.

But somewhere in the dark before dawn a six-year old lay shivering with cold, and very scared in that black tunnel. Sleep must have overtaken her for there was a nudge at her arm and when she opened her eyes she saw a big shaggy dog with round sad eyes. He pawed at her sleeve and lay down beside her, giving her little body his warmth -- she clinging to him as though he were Nanny. The mangy creature got up and went to the entrance of the pipe, setting up a barking that would have awakened the dead. Well, it finally did wake up a dozing bobby not far away who came flying over to capture the beast. The dog ran back into the tube, continuing to howl, while chased by the officer -- and there was Rose singing softly the Sunday School song, "Lead Kingly Light." She only knew a few lines... "The night is dark, and I am far from home -- Lead Thou me on!" which she sang over and over many times. (Nanny had taken her to church every Sunday.)

The officer had soothed and eased her out to the fresh air. "So you're the little girl who ran from home!" "Yes, Sir, I was looking for my friend and I got lost."

She was taken to her home where much

thanksgiving was celebrated -- and the officer congratulated on finding her. Rose turned round and round looking for the shaggy dog and told her father that the *dog* had saved her by fetching the police. So, Mr. Edleigh spoke more harshly to the young 'bobbie' and commanded him to find the dog, which wasn't difficult, as he had not ceased following them... slinking in the underbrush all the way to Rose's home. He was brought in and given food, combed and treated royally -- but not Rose! Though thankful for her rescue, *her* reception was not so regal. Nice little girls didn't run away from home! So the housekeeper put her in the tub, scrubbed her hair (and not too gently), pulled her nightie over her shoulders and down her frail little body. "To bed with you, young lady!"

As she lay there, more lonely than she was before they found her... the door cracked, and in slunk the shaggy dog. He jumped on the bed and curled up at her feet. All was right with the world now... but where was Nanny? Her father said he would call the veterinarian and find out who the dog belonged to... and see about getting a medal for the dog's achievement. It turned out that the dog was known by a numbered tag around his neck. On communicating with the dog's owner, Mr. Edleigh was told, even begged, to keep the dog if he wanted... he had never been happy with them, as the brute was a child lover. So there was great rejoicing by all.

The next day some decisions were to be made for Rose's schooling. With the big household not running smoothly: the new chef, the rather unqualified governess, and the unhappy child who wanted nothing much more than playing like the Chopin she had heard. Something must be done. Fire the governess, find

Nanny, re-hire the old cook, Begonia. It wasn't going to be easy. Governess Plimpsted didn't take it calmly, but Father gave her good recommendations (with a twitch of his conscience) and an extra month's pay. He found Nanny living with her aged brother, and under the new arrangements at Edleigh House, she was happy to rejoin our family. She was to live permanently with us -- even after Rose was grown up. Fortunately, Cook came back. We could hear her coming up the driveway with all her pots and pans jangling in the back of the carriage.

Nanny suggested that with Rose's gift for learning, she herself could coach her and let her develop at her own pace. The library's four walls were filled from ceiling to floor with enough books to see one through several University degrees. Rose was already stealing forbidden peeks into some of John Henry Newman's writings. She had first known about him from her favorite hymn, "Lead Kingly Light." Once she asked Nanny to read her to sleep and pulled out from under her bed Newman's "The Dream of Gerontius." Nanny hesitated -- then after scanning a few lines she thought -- why not?

By the time she reached the halfway point...

Softly and gently, dearly-ransomed soul,
In my most loving arms I now enfold thee,
And o'er the penal water, as they roll,
I poise thee and I lower thee, and hold thee...

Rose had fallen asleep. Peace settled in at Edleigh House.

And days rocked on... Rose was not liking Bach's music. "It doesn't sound nice." "But it's for study, dear. By following the given fingering, you can master technical problems that will come later."

Next year I'd be ready for two-part inventions. My academic level was up to eighth form, and I liked algebra. Father was satisfied with the way things were getting along in the household. So all was right with the world!

My seventh birthday came, but remembering last year's fiasco, I opted to go to the opera with Father instead of a party. Rossini's *The Barber of Seville* was playing -- produced by a London Company at the Orpheum. And I thought it was the greatest thing I'd ever seen. There was one laugh after another. When it was over, we went backstage and met some of the singers. The youngest soprano was Joanna from Germany, a niece of Richard Wagner. (Wagner had just completed his opera *Lohengrin* that was sweeping the musical world.) I was so enchanted that I hummed the arias most all the way home, which took a long time in going from the opera house, in the heart of London, to Hampstead. Father carried Rose who had long since slipped into dreamland. No sooner was she laid in her bed than in crept Barnabus -- so named because of his similarity to a St. Bernard dog. He took his place at her feet.

Morning tiptoed in on little beams of sunshine across her room. It was Sunday and Rose asked Nanny if they could go to church, and she was pleased at the suggestion; she had not been off the estate in such a long time. "Let's go to St. Pancras -- it's not too far

from Euston Station, and afterwards we might take
lunch at a little Victorian hotel across the street. You
know what! It would be a good day to visit the Tower
of London, since we have been reading about the kings
of England."

Rose was delighted... and the day was perfect. St.
Pancras Church was a new one, having been completed
in 1822 -- only thirty years ago. Since they were also
studying Greek architecture, it would be a good exam-
ple, as it was decorated with caryatids of the
Erechtheum Temple on the Acropolis. The sculptor
had made plaster casts of the original figures which he
then turned into terracotta copies. These were placed
so that they concealed the true cast-iron columns. It
was all so wonderful. Then they hired a cabby to drive
them to the Tower of London where they saw the col-

lection of Tudor uniforms -- Nanny explaining every-thing as they went along. "You know King Henry's daughter, Bess, was the last of the Tudors when she died in 1603," and then she showed her St. Edward's crown... "he was called the 'Confessor'." Lastly, they went to the sad little plot where so many of royalty were executed... even Queen Elizabeth's own mother.

On the way home, Nanny told Rose that she thought it was time a little gaiety was brought to their house -- how would she like her to plan a tea party for next Sunday? "Will I be asked to play?" asked the little 'born ham.'

"I will make sure of that... in fact, the Scarlatti Sonata is in good shape and follow that with your own nice composition. I believe our guests will enjoy that very much." Father liked the idea, there had not been enough laughter around the place for a young girl... other than the mischief she cooked up herself.

Nanny had more in mind than pouring tea from a Wedgwood pot -- she was thinking that Mr. John Edleigh had been long enough without a mate -- and how Rose needed a complete family. Soon she would be nine, and Nanny herself was growing tired; that pain in her side was more constant these days, but she said nothing about it.

The invitation list was made up. The first names were the Althorpes and their beautiful niece who was spending several months with them before they were to leave the country for India. Next would be the Black-stones and their ten year old daughter; the Wheatons; the Reverend Mr. Bertram Aston; and lastly the Smith-ertons. Cook had been toiling for days planning the food: raspberry jam, clotted cream, scones, strawber-ries, sesame seed cake, charlotte russe and, of course, pots and pots of steaming tea. The tables were put in the garden, covered with the finest Irish linen cloths. Pink roses and blue delphiniums were arranged in crystal vases. The day was perfect and the borders of the house frontage were a riot of colorful rhododendrons... dark red, purple, and yellow!

At four o'clock the first guests arrived... the Althorpes and Carnelia, their nineteen year old kin. Rose had never seen such a pretty young lady; what blue eyes, the color of the blue ribbon that tied back her light brown curls. Soon everyone appeared and all the drivers had been sent to the back where a long trestle table was set for the domestics and chauffeurs.

When all the appetites were satisfied, they arose and followed their host into the drawing room. Mr. Edleigh announced that it was his pleasure to present his daughter Rose to play for them. There was a profusion of compliments and requests for encores. Rose was satisfied that she had pleased her father, and threw her arms around him. Miss Carnelia took her in her arms and told her how wonderful to have someone close by who could play accompaniment to her violin. A new day had come to Edleigh House; Carnelia promised to bring the music scores by the next day so she would be prepared for their duet sessions.

That night Nanny went to bed happy, knowing everything was headed right. Her scheme was working. It just wasn't natural that a handsome man of twenty-eight should live in this big house without a companion. She fell asleep quickly. Rose's music was showing maturity... more discipline had been required to do the accompaniments for Miss Carnelia. It would be grand when she returned for another nice visit... since her uncle had postponed his India trip for a year. They could resume their music together. And 'Father' -- it was never 'Papa' anymore, now that she kept company with a grown-up lady -- was looking younger than ever. He planned more time at home, where he could watch his daughter and the lovely violinist in their practice sessions.

And one day Rose just came out in her candid way and asked Carnelia if she liked her father. Carnelia blushed terribly all the way down her neck, and answered just as candidly, "Yes, Rose, I do." Rose leaped from the piano and ran to Mr. Edleigh, "Pa -- Father, Miss Carnelia likes you! You *do* like *her*, don't you?"

Father walked up to Carnelia and asked if this were true? The answer was in her eyes. There were tears in his eyes, too. "Shall we skip all the preliminaries and get on with our lives?" Again, the answer was in those beautiful blue orbs. Shall we have Rose play our wedding song?"

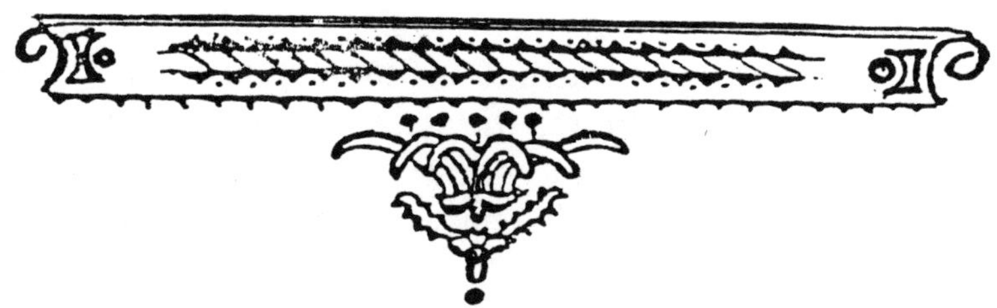

Carnelia needed to go into London for a few wardrobe items and they set the date for the next Wednesday... If the Reverend Mr. Aston could perform their ceremony. He could -- and it was just fine with the shaggy Barnabus. He even let them put a white bow around his neck. The services were held in the drawing room with only the household and the Althorpes to witness. Nanny looked all right, but she wouldn't be able to hold that smile much longer. She was seeing the happy results of her long and patient plotting. The new Mrs. Edleigh and her flustered groom decided to take a run down to Dorset for a fortnight. This seacoast town of Bournemouth was just becoming a popular resort on the English Channel. It had been only a fishing village until about 1810. Now royalty was discovering it's salubrious air and lovely chines -- as those undulating cliffs on the embankment were called. In a few years, Queen Victoria would be spending her leisure time at the *Royal Bath* -- and inviting her dear friend, Disraeli, to 'take the water' there.

As they strolled the promenade, the splendid newly weds had heads turning to better view them as they passed the milling resortists. When they sat on the sandy beach, Carnelia took John's hand and said, "Dear, you know nothing about me, do you? -- and I know all about you from my uncle's constant praise of you. I am very rich through my inheritance, but I'd give it all in a blink of an eye to further Rose's development in her music. You do not seem to realize she's no ordinary child -- she must have the best available teachers. There is an Academy for Young Ladies opening up here in Bournemouth and when she is old enough, we will be unselfish enough to let her seek her destiny... unless you have other things in mind. Nanny has given her all she can... and I know she is ill."

The next day Father and Carnelia were to return to Hampstead. The house was spotless; there were

flowers from the garden adorning every room to welcome them home.

"Can we set up the wickets for a game on the side
yard?" asked Rose. "Well, dear, I think they will be
rather tired after that long trip... perhaps the next day."

"And you will play with us?" The child could not
know how Nanny was suffering with her malady these
late days. Nanny thought she would spare her as long
as she could.

Upton, the stable caretaker, would pick the new
Mr. and Mrs. Edleigh up at Euston Station and bring
them home in the new fashionable carriage. Carnelia
was radiant and her husband was bursting with pride.
She really was a stranger to the intimate parts of the
house, and was pleased they were being placed in the
front upstairs room with the view of the pond and gardens. They had been greeted at the door by Cook,
Miss Manners the housekeeper, and old Peter the gardener. "It was time this manor had a mistress," said the
latter, "Welcome to the grounds."

"Thank you all; this is the happiest time I've ever known. Now we are all a family." Shaggy Barnabus wagging his approval, gave three barks, interrupting the rest of Carnelia's speech.

Regularity settled down in the residence, and Rose and Carnelia continued their music sessions. Soon they were being noticed by all Hampstead for their professionalism. Rose was allowed much freedom to explore the community as long as Barnabus was with her. He clung to her like a shadow. She ventured as far as the southeast corner of town known as Keats Grove, where the poet John Keats had spent a while with his friend, Charles Armitage Brown. Next door his sweetheart was living; she inspired Keats in writing his immortal poems. Rose enjoyed Nanny reading his "Eve of St. Agnes," all about a saint who was martyred in Rome in the year 300 on St. Agnes' Day (January 21). There grew a legend in the middle ages that on St. Agnes' Eve (January 20), a girl could find out who her future husband would be if she placed both hands beneath her head as she lay on her back. He will appear before her in a dream and kiss her. Rose loved to have Nanny read this to her before she went to sleep. She even memorized parts of it:

> They told her how, upon St. Agnes' Eve
> Young virgins might have visions of delight
> And soft adorings from their loves receive
> Upon the honeyed middle of the night.

Mostly, the reader thought it was the rhythm of the meter. Then one night the little girl suddenly asked Nanny, "How can I be a virgin, Nanny?"

Oh... oh, the time had come for that little 'lady talk' that she knew would be facing her soon. She replied, unable to cope with the problem, "Just stay like you are, my sweet, we will talk tomorrow."

"Nanny, when Keats says, 'A thing of beauty is a joy forever,' does it mean that a piece of music is written and its melody keeps coming back to you forever -- and is as beautiful as the first time?" "Yes, dear, goodnight."

CHAPTER 2

- 1852-

The Royal Exchange where Mr. Edleigh was connected was tied up in London for the time being -- rumors were flying. Trouble was brewing in foreign trade. There was also much upheaval in Parliament. The Tory Party had been split up back in 1846, which had upset Queen Victoria. Lord Palmerston was a Whig and he firmly believed in Constitutional restraints on Monarchs. Victoria disliked his policy and his methods both. The average Britisher put his trust in 'Pam', as they affectionally called him. Lord Russell was Prime Minister; his job was not easy: soothing the friction and keeping peace between the Queen and her foreign Minister. Lord John Russell finally told Palmerston that he must keep the angry Queen informed on every move, and show her more respect... or England was going to suffer. The basic trouble was that Victoria could not accept the fact that the foreign policy had slipped out of the hands of the Crown and into the hands of the Commons -- and that the Foreign Secretary could pay little attention to Royal advice if he pleased.

By 1851 France had elected Louis Napoleon (Bonaparte's nephew) to be President of the New Republic. Three years previously Louis Philippe and the Royal Family had been expelled from France. The Queen of England and Lord John Russell agreed England should stay out of those matters, but soon learned that Lord Palmerston, taking things in his own hands, had assured the French Ambassador of English support. The British Government found they could not endure a house-divided. So the Queen had to accept Palmerston as Home Secretary -- which at least meant he would no longer be at the Foreign Office!

A new crisis was stalking by 1853: there was a growing weakness in the sprawling empire of the Turks.

"Do you understand any of this, Rose, dear?" asked Nanny.

"A little, but not much. I just saw on the front page of the *London Times* that troops are being sent to the Crimea -- war has been declared. Then it told all about Florence Nightingale and the nurses that cared for the injured soldiers. Gosh, I wish I could be a nurse!"

"Well you're much too young yet and besides, what about your piano? You haven't forgotten your dream of a concert career, have you?"

"No, Nanny, but they treat the poor soldiers so badly, while they sell commissions to the rich men. I don't think that's fair!"

It was almost yule season. Two years had passed in happiness with the new Mrs. Edleigh, but by now Nanny was old and weak. They had fixed her room up on the sunniest side of the house where the windows were wide and as much cheer as could be mustered up was brought into her quarters. Rose sat at her bedside and asked her darling old friend, "*en qui puesto servirle, Nannacita; et que'tal le gusta mi español*. I am studying very had to learn Spanish, because I'd like to go to Spain some day."

"I will talk to your father and mother about your

entering a Girl's Academy. I hear there is a fine one in Bournemouth -- though that's awfully far from here. Would you like to go away to school?"

"Yes, I think so. But what would I do about the piano? Would there be some one there that would teach music?"

"There is a music department, but if it doesn't prove satisfactory we can apply for lessons in London every other weekend. And besides that will give your parents more time to be with you. The time has come to tell you, my sweet child, my end is near. Don't cry, Rose. Stop it! You know it must come to everyone. You have been my life here, and now it's time to turn you over to others. *Hasta luego, nina mia linda.*"

Rose crept out of the room. She knew in her heart that this was the last time she would see this grand old lady again. She looked for Carnelia to see if she felt like playing the Gounod-Bach "Ave Maria." And such music they made -- the melody flowed into Nanny's room where she climbed from bed to her knees for her last prayer.

Cook found her there when she brought her supper tray. Preparations were quiet and simple. They held a wake for her in the drawing room, and Rose and Carnelia played soft music -- all the time "*hasta luego, nina mia linda*" burning in Rose's ear. "And I didn't know her real name!" "It was Melia Porter -- her family is dead, and we've been all she had since before you were born," said Father.

Melia was buried in the Parish Church yard -- you could spot her grave from a distance -- the one with all the fresh flowers every day, picked by Rose at Edleigh House. Barnabus occasionally took long naps on the grassy mound, for soon he, too, would be joining her new world -- maybe a different one, but whatever kind of world pets go to.

Christmas came and went. January was mild, at least the first week of it was. A young man that Rose had spotted before, approached their house and turned in their lane. When the butler (they had acquired one, now that Nanny was here no longer) answered the knock. The fellow introduced himself as George du Maurier, apologized profusely for his intrusion, but could not help asking about the marvelous music that he heard each time he passed the house. Sims asked him to step inside and he would summon the Master. Mr. Edleigh was delighted to receive him. He had heard about his musical and painting accomplishments from a neighbor. Would he stay and listen to the music, and tea would be in shortly.   He declined tea, but "another time would be pleasant." So a little party was scheduled for next Sunday. The Reverend Mr. Aston accepted, as did several others.   Mr. du Maurier seemed about twenty or so and very genial. The Reverend announced that George had a wonderfully melodic voice... and, of course, a request was responded to. It was the "Ave Maria" -- a bad choice, as before it was finished, Rose was in tears and made a dash for her room. Then Carnelia explained that it was her Nanny's favorite song, that she had just died.

Mr. Aston asked George about his career. George told him that his father had great aspirations for him as a scientist -- that was why they had moved to London where his father's invention of a portable lamp might be better received. But, as for himself, he wanted to be an artist.

While Rose was out of the room, indulging her flood of grief, her schooling was brought up and the idea of the Bournemouth Girl's Academy was thought the best thing for her. She could try it for a year, anyway.

With the coming of fall, Barnabus was laid to rest in the garden -- Rose had conducted his funeral rites between sobs, but finally accepted the inevitable. Next week she would leave for Dorset where her first formal schooling would begin. After certain academic tests... she was placed high on the form list. Her classes in language, history and math would be in the same group with the seventeen year oldsters, though she was only fourteen. Chemistry would be new to her, though. The girls were charming in their school uniforms, and she rather liked the way she looked, too. It'll be such fun going back to Hampstead and wearing something different from any body else. Her music teacher was sufficient for the time being. She was the pianist for the school orchestra.

On her first trip home, she found that Mr. Louis-Maturin du Maurier had died and that his son, George, had returned to Paris to pursue his dreams. It was good to see her father and Carnelia again, and so happy --, gave her a sense of security. After two years at Bournemouth, she was graduated first in her class, also youngest. Her life moved on with the rhythm of the music she loved so much. It was decided by all now, that she needed some eminent music teacher. She went to audition for Dr. Walter C. MacFarren, composer and pianist. Needless to say, MacFarren was overjoyed to accept her as a pupil. As she was only sixteen she would commute by train to London, first going to Finchley Station, then St. John's Wood and on to Baker Street for her lesson. Rose made progress by leaps and bounds. It was now 1860.

Walter MacFarren was a protégée of Ferdinand Hiller (born of German-Jewish parents in Frankfurt) -- and, like Hiller, he believed in hard work. He immediately liked the sensitivity of Rose's personality. "No amount of labor or zest can make up for the lack of this personal quality -- and no amount of personality can make up for the lack of hard practice!" he preached constantly -- "and the hardest member of the hand to deal with is the thumb, but the most precious of all. It demands a muscular action entirely different from merely pressing down a key with any other finger." (This Rose knew from long hours with Nanny.) He would not permit her to appear before any audience until she was thoroughly ready. "You do not wish to be exposed to criticism by performing prematurely -- or to be displayed like a talented ape in a circus, do you? -- thus we *learn*, we *think*, we *work*; then your audience will be there!"

So, from 1860 until 1863 Rose made her weekly trek from Hampstead Heath to Baker Street in London. During the week she and Carnelia played duets. They had the Beethoven *Sonata in F for Violin and Piano* down to a Queen's taste; and despite her piano teacher's advice on acrobatic 'simians', she and Carnelia were going to present it to the public at the soirée at Kenwood House. Kenwood is in a large park thick with oaks and beaches, it was remodeled in neo-Classical style in the late eighteenth century. Many summer concerts were given there. She rather hoped MacFarren wouldn't hear about it. He *did*! We were asked to render it to him at his studio... a command performance of a different kind. Carnelia and I complied at my next lesson... I, feeling like I'd been sent to the principal's office for some infraction of rules.

He was elated! "Remarkable, marvelous, bravo!" he repeated several times. "I will arrange for you to play at Buckingham Palace. The Queen will be delighted -- she loves her subjects dearly."

"Mrs. Edleigh, I would like to talk with you alone." They withdrew, leaving Rose at the keyboard. "I don't know how you feel about your daughter going to study in Europe, but there's a man, Karl Tausig... a young man who studied under Franz Liszt... he isn't much older than Rose, but he has founded a school in Berlin for young artists such as Rose. Talk with her father about it, and on his approval I can make arrangements for her. I can teach her nothing more -- I must be honest with you. She has been the joy of my teaching profession -- the world is waiting for her finishing touches."

They played for the Queen, the Royal Family, the Royal Dukes, the Royal Duchesses, and the Royal servants -- who stood in the Royal butler's quarters. It was thrilling -- after this what greater thing could happen -- 'cept having Nanny here.

Finishing a late supper on the day of the last lesson, Carnelia talked to her husband concerning Rose's going to Germany and got a real surprise when John said that perhaps a trip abroad would be a good thing for them all.

"But we must let MacFarren know of our plans if he is to recommend Rose as a student. Why don't we ask him to set up an appointment with Tausig to hear her play -- and just take it from there."

Then Mr. Edleigh got serious about political conditions in Germany with Bismarck and Napoleon putting their heads together. "Look at what's going on in Mexico; Napoleon and Franz-Josef cooking up something in Mexico. It has been rumored that the Emperor of Austria has in mind to send his brother Maximilian to be head of the Mexicans -- and look how Napoleon has failed to intervene in Poland on the side of the patriotic rebels. I just don't trust the way things are going on over there."

"Well, she would be in a world apart from all that -- can't we just go and see for ourselves what the conditions are?" offered Carnelia.

Things got buzzing around the Edleigh household... what to take, transportation reservations, where to stay... so much to do! But they were off within the fortnight. The train would get them to Dover, then across the Channel to Ostend, through northern Belgium, then enter Germany and go straight to Berlin. It seemed an awful long way to go, but the trains were so comfortable.

Arriving in Berlin station they took a cab -- somewhat like the old hansom back home that they called the 'Gondola of London.' There were trunks and trunks laden with crinoline dresses with hoops in the skirts -- and of course a bonnet for each one. The driver was given an address on Nonnendammalle -- none dared to pronounce it. It was respectable looking, but Rose asked how on earth they could ever talk to people in this impossible language. Mr. Edleigh explained they would hire a language student to translate for them. The driver turned to the family and said he knew English thoroughly... had studied at Oxford University. So that problem was settled.

The next day they were to meet Herr Tausig; his studio was not far from their hotel. On the way over to their appointment, they passed close to the Schloss Charlottenburg. "How charming," exclaimed Rose. The translator, whose name was Fritz, said there were many beautiful and breath-taking things to see in Berlin. "The Charlottenburg Castle was begun in 1695, on a location selected by Sophie Charlotte, the first Queen of Prussia. We must explore it when you get settled," said Fritz. "That will be wonderful," she beamed at the shy young German. He would get in touch with her tomorrow.

CHAPTER 3

Mid Eighteen-Sixties

There was war waging in Germany and there were husbands of two of Queen Victoria's daughters positioned on opposite sides of politics. Most of the activity was being carried on in the vicinity of Darmstadt. Austria was utterly bested in the conflict; Prussia annexed Hanover, Hesse-Cassel and others as victory spoils. But if any of this existed, it was unknown in Rose's world of music and enthusiasm of the beauty around her.

She and her parents called on Herr Tausig who was ready to receive her because of the glowing letter from her former teacher in London. Her classes were started the next day. John and Carnelia got her established in a boarding house for young ladies, close enough that Rose could walk to lessons. What amazed her most was that so many Germans could speak English.

Soon tearful goodbyes were exchanged and Rose was alone for the first time in her life. She had forgotten the nice young German student that had been their guide, what with so much to grasp on to... great was her surprise when she answered the knock at her door and it was Fritz. "Am I interrupting your work? If so, I can come back again." She replied that it would be best, as she was involved with preparing her assignment for the

Professor. But there was a mutual sparkle in two pairs of eyes.

At her first session, she found that the language presented very little problem, for with music there are so many cognates that it's almost a universal language in itself. Herr Tausig assigned her all the major and minor scales played in octaves, thirds, fifths, and tenths; the First Prelude in the *Well-Tempered Clavichord*, and one number from her memorized repertoire. The piano at her disposal at the boarding house was not up to what she desired, but would do.

"So hungry am I for some wonderful Chopin Sonata that I will work six hours a day on my assignment to show Herr Tausig I can do it!" she wrote her parents.

Already she had completed the A major "Militarie Polonaise" of Chopin -- but did not care much for it; Tausig advised more Beethoven first, specifically the *Pathétique*. And she did as she was told. As the work progressed, she became very fond of it -- especially the slow Adagio Cantabile movement. "I would rather you practice three hours of good work than six hours of daydreaming at the keyboard," he said. "Get more fresh air and sunshine. You can go nowhere without good health."

It was decided that she was to study German, so with the piano practice and the language she would still have time to see some of the sights of Berlin. Fritz came to her place a week later and asked her if she'd like to go to a concert. Hans von Bülow who had been a pupil of Friedrich Wieck and Franz Liszt, but now a director of the Conservatory at Munich, was giving a performance at the Palace Concert Hall. Rose was delighted. There she saw her professor who had known von Bülow when their paths had crossed many times at

Liszt's studio. That night, Rose found it hard to fall asleep... was it the music, the exhilaration of the concert hall or was it Fritz? Twenty-three was high time a girl noticed a fellow! He spoke so seldom of himself that she found it hard to know him well. He lived in Nürnberg; his parents ran a small business; he was in Berlin to study architecture. Fritz asked if it would disturb the maestro if he accompanied her to her next lesson. She thought it wouldn't -- "just come anyway and if he prefers not, you can just sit outside and listen."

The following Friday, Fritz met Rose at the appointed hour outside the teacher's studio. She rang his bell, "Herr Tausig, this is Fritz Rhinhardt, my translator and friend." With Fritz right there she was better able to explain her dislike for the Chopin "A Major Polonaise."

"Ach, I see," interpreted Fritz, "you do not understand the music. It's a picture of Poland's greatness. I am Polish. I *feel* the composition... it is the best known and most muscular of all of his dances. There was a story that ran thus: after composing this piece Chopin was terrified in the sleepless dreary night -- he thought he saw ghosts of Polish nobles and richly dressed ladies slowly move by him. He was so troubled that he fled his apartment in the Château at Nohant, but he immediately took up his pen and began to complete the brilliant opus as soon as he could reach an all-night cafe. It is a magnificent piece and I'd like you to resume work on it. You have the hands for its demands."

The teacher was pleased with her scale work and the Bach. She had selected one of her own compositions from her repertoire to play for him, but made up a composer's name. "Now, my friend, that was the loveliest melody I've heard in a long time, but it wasn't written by your 'Carlo Passo' -- you composed it yourself -- did you not? Why do you not claim it! It was splendid -- I was lost in clouds for the moment while you played. We must do something about your creativity. And for your next lesson: scales as usual and arpeggios... as for the Beethoven *Pathétique*, I should like you to take only a phrase at a time, hands separately, five times each, then together five times. Watch all expression marks, use the metronome... gradually bringing up the speed to its correct timing. Then play that phrase from memory. Proceed to the next... etc... and listen, listen and listen: if *you* don't -- nobody *else* will! Good day, Fritz, good day, Rose."

"Thank you, Herr Tausig," and out they tripped into the glorious crisp air. Fritz was radiant -- he admitted to playing oboe -- "and not badly." "Oh, that's wonderful, I love the oboe. We must learn something together and surprise my teacher," said she.

"And he'll be sending me a bill, too," replied he.

There were frequent letters from Hampstead.

"The rhododendrons are more beautiful than ever. A new nest of robins has moved in the elm by your window. The Queen is very concerned over the increasing number of accidents which had lately occurred on many lines of railroads. She hoped she would not have to carry the matter of the heavy responsibility, which they have assumed, since they have succeeded in acquiring the monopoly of the vogue of traveling of almost the entire population of the country." He wrote of the assassination of the American President Abraham Lincoln, and how the Queen had written by hand, a note of condolence to the widow. "In August, the Queen will visit in Germany at Rosenau, and then on to Coburg where the birthday of the Prince Consort will be celebrated by the erecting of a costly monument to his memory. Carnelia and I enjoy your letters about your musical progress and language study. We are glad you have found a friend in Fritz, as he seemed quite genteel. Your loving Father and Mother."

Rose was settling down to a regular schedule of early rising, breakfast, one and a half hour's practice, a walk around several blocks -- different ones each time, an hour of German grammar and vocabulary, light lunch, short siesta and back to the piano for another hour on the *Pathétique*. The rest of the day was spent in caring for her clothes, writing letters, or reading. She'd give almost anything for a good cup of tea and a scone, a Dorset dumpling, or Yorkshire pudding! Homesickness came over her. So she took up her pen and began writing:

My Dearest Father and Mother,

I miss home so much today. Couldn't you take off and come to Berlin, please. I will surprise you with what Fritz and I have learned to play. Maestro says we are splendid together, and thinks we should get a clarinetist and violinist to form a quartet. They will meet here as that is the only place with a piano. Couldn't you make it for Christmas?

Fritz's parents will visit him next week and he wants me to meet them.

All for now.

Love, Rose

CHAPTER 4

Back in England, the letter having arrived four days later -- John Edleigh had decided that he and Carnelia would be taking a trip to Berlin *sooner* than Christmas! Young Fritz's name was cropping up an awful lot of times. Besides, Rose was playing a recital with two other musicians and they were anxious to hear her. So the middle of November was decided upon.

The Rhinhardts were now in Berlin, and a day later Fritz asked Rose to join him and his parents at the Tiergarten for lunch. The parents were reassured that they should just relax, that Rose was a nice, sensible, talented girl. He told his reluctant mother to take a headache powder and simply act like she was only the girl next door! The trouble *was* that she *wasn't* the 'girl next door.' Frau and Herr Rhinhardt and their neighbors, the Engles, had already 'cooked-up' a family alliance between Fritz and their daughter without informing either of their offspring.

Herr Rhinhardt hailed a hansom and gave him the address for Rose Edleigh's place of residence. After the round of introductions of Fritz's parents to Rose, they seated themselves in the carriage and off to the park. The mother kept eyeing the English girl up and down. By now Rose had spent almost a year in

Berlin and was able to handle a few nice phrases in German. 'Big Mama' was all ears for every little glance between her son and his friend. And all they could talk about was music, music, music! The afternoon was spent in pleasure for Papa, son and Rose, but Mama couldn't quite get it all... boy and girl on equal basis -- no sweet talk... no trying to sneak behind a tree. Well... we'll keep our eyes open!, thought the old lady -- almost out loud.

They didn't meet again. Mother and son had a long talk that evening and she told him the plans that had been made. He would finish at the University in the spring and would return to Nürnberg to go into business with one of his father's friends. She deferred speaking of the little conjugal scheming that was in store for the not-too-far away nuptials.

When Fritz was free again, he came to Rose's residence for a practice session. He hoped she liked his family. "Just lovely -- smashing, Fritz."

For the first time he laid his hand on hers and told her of the plans for his career that were being made for him. "I think that's wonderful -- no job hunting and applications to fill out for a hundred possible openings. I am very happy for you..." and he broke off her sentence with "What about *us*, Rose?"

"I didn't know there was anything about *us* except we are very good friends and enjoy one another's company." Whereupon he bent over and kissed her square upon the lips. Rose didn't flinch or pull back, though no one had ever done that but Father or Nanny. "Rose, you are blushing --" said Fritz. "Well, let's do it again -- I promise I *won't* this time," she laughed.

The door opened to the music room -- "Oops, sorry," said her roommate, as she handed Rose the letter from her father.

"Do you mind if I open it, I'm dying to hear from England."

"Take your time and I'll be warming up 'Obie' with scales before the others get here," replied Fritz.

The letter said that Mr. and Mrs. Edleigh would be arriving on November 20th in time for the musical. Everything was fine in Hampstead. "Do you remember the young George du Maurier who would come and sing to us with his golden voice?"

Rose closed her eyes and relived those ecstatic moments when, before a small audience in their drawing room, George would sing "Du Lieben Langen Tag" -- it was like gazing across the sea in moonlight, hearing the rippling waves falling on the shore. "Mr. du Maurier has returned from Paris and lives in Hampstead Heath with his wife, Emma, an English girl. He fell into a fortunate position with *Punch Weekly*, a very well-perused publication... even Parliament and the Queen turn first to the cartoon section and sit up taking notice. Du Maurier's drawings are editorials themselves. I understand he is writing on a novel, also.

"Well, we placed flowers on Nanny's grave as it would have been her 85th birthday. We will see you before you know it. Lovingly, Father ('Papa' I like better)" -- said his P.S.

Rose folded the letter and placed it in her pocket. "Are you through with your warm-up? I wish you knew what England was like... and I want you to meet my family in November."

Fritz expressed desire to do so. "Who else is on the program with you?"

"Well, there will be Oscar Bolk... he's a genius, then Lilly Lehmann has a group of German songs and I'm last. Tausig wants me to do two Bach Preludes from *The Well-Tempered Clavichord*, followed by my own composition "Tintagel Rhapsody." And you will come, won't you, Fritz?" "Rose, you know I wouldn't miss it!"

"I mustn't see much of you the next few weeks; I feel I need more practice. So at the concert, then?"

The clarinetist came in, but the violinist couldn't make it. They selected some Mozart -- all sight-reading their parts. The session was surprisingly good. Their next practice would be after her recital.

Rose had a peculiar night; sleep wouldn't come; she couldn't go to the piano at this hour of the night and work off her emotions. She realized she was missing something -- so she slipped from her bed and fell on her knees to talk it over with her Lord. "I feel insecure, what is wrong -- where am I failing -- I know I have not attended church since leaving home, but I don't believe that can be it, since You are here with me constantly. I trust You to show me the way. Is it Fritz? Amen."

     Next morning she had over-slept and missed breakfast. She dressed and walked to the corner where she knew of a small cafe. After that -- back to the piano. Practice was inspired -- two hours passed before she felt the slightest fatigue. German class was after lunch time and that went well. Rose decided to walk to the old church Gedächtniskirche with the fine tower. Fritz had told her about its architectural beauty. She found the Kurfurstendamm -- the street where it was located -- and being a good British walker she finally came upon it centering an intersection of four streets. Oh! So beautiful it was... but not like her own West-minister Abbey or the great domed building of St. Paul's Cathedral with its honest and straight-forward classical lines. She chose another route for returning to her quarters, and upon arriving found a large parcel addressed to her. Hastily she ran to her room, plopped it on the bed and tore open the package. Ooooh... what a glorious thing lay folded in the tissues! She held it up to the mirror and looked at her reflection. It was pearl-colored silk crinoline with yards and yards of gathering at the waistline that fell to the floor in a modified hoopskirt, flounces were caught up in dark green velvet ribbon. The back of the skirt trailed the floor too much. She slipped it on... a perfect fit 'cept the length. How could Carnelia have known her size, then she remembered they wore the same. There were matching slippers; she bent over to try them... gracious! The hem of the dress that held the hoop flopped up and hit her on the forehead. What to do! Imagine her coming on stage and sitting at the piano and the dress flying over her head. Rose laughed at the imaginary scene.

Louisa came into the room and, extracting her from all the folderol, announced that her voice teacher was presenting the advanced students in a pre-Christmas concert. Louisa was from Canada; it was wonderful to have someone to chat with in English. "Gee, Rose, wherever did you get that gorgeous frock?"... and Rose said, "Would you like to wear it to your program? What can I do about this skirt to keep it from swallowing me up when I sit to play?" Louisa suggested taking the wire out. "It will make it longer -- and I think it will be even prettier. We can catch up more in the loops of ribbon and shorten the front and let the back trail a bit more."

"How clever you are" -- and Rose began snipping the wire... "We can replace the hoops for some other occasion."

After removing the dress and hanging it up they both lay back on their beds for some 'girl talk'. "Louisa, has a boy ever kissed you?"

"Now, why would you ask me a question like that! -- I know -- You and Fritz! Do you love him? I've been watching you two when you played music together."

"I don't know just what love is except I love my parents, my God, -- my music -- but this doesn't feel the same. I think it's like my father loves Carnelia."

"Look out, Rose, you better slow this business down -- you know how things are going on in this country. He's a German to the core... and you're the most English of the English!"

"Well, I've told Fritz I will not see him until after my performance. My parents will be here by then...

that gives me time to clear my head."

The days passed by seeing a more serious Rose than ever before. She was on a new work of Franz Liszt, her teacher's teacher. The *Un Sospiro* was difficult reading -- but the technical demands did not exceed her ability. The memorizing was easy -- in fact that was the only way one could play it, as the eye had to focus on the hands so much. Rose obtained all the information she could about this astonishing composer, and pleased Herr Tausig by discussing his own teacher with him.

The great day came. Mr. and Mrs. Edleigh arrived in Berlin and went straight to see Rose. It was the twentieth of November and the ground was covered with snow; icicles jingled together like chimes in the wind. Parents and daughter clung together in an embrace that a hurricane would find hard to tear apart. "Come to my room, I want you to meet my friend Louisa. She is most clever and sings like a nightingale. Her German is better than mine as she's been here since she was little. Her parents were in the Embassy."

CHAPTER 5

In the interim since Fritz had seen Rose, he had received word from home. He sweated as he read the letter. His mother had not 'taken to' his last tidings. There were too many references to that English girl they had met while visiting their son in Berlin. Frau Rhinhardt sang praises about Elsa, the girl next door. They would be expecting him home for Christmas. "There are to be many parties -- the first at *Elsa's* beautiful home. *Elsa* is a wonderful cook! *Elsa* makes her own gorgeous clothes. *Elsa* is looking forward to your homecoming." Fritz dashed the letter down -- he could see through the whole thing! His mother and her schemes! So, it was Elsa's father that had offered the position to Fritz with his company. Well, he wouldn't concern himself anymore with that mess. Tomorrow was Rose's concert -- it had been so long since he had seen her!

He went to his wardrobe and looked over his best suit, brushed it up a bit and selected the right ascot. Hours were spent polishing his shoes and laying out his clothes for the event. He found himself being very nervous about the entire thing: meeting her family again -- maybe they brought her boyfriend -- how could he know... they'd never discussed anything like that. He was frightened for her playing -- he had everything going wrong: maybe he didn't get the correct hour for the recital; perhaps his cab might break down; he couldn't think of anything else right now to scare him to death... but that would do for the time being. He took out his oboe to calm himself, but after a few bars his neighbor in the next room started to banging on the wall telling him to 'knock it off'! So he went out for a walk, his breath solidifying before him in the sub-freezing weather -- never had it been this cold in November.

Tomorrow came. He leisurely bathed, dressed, and left two hours earlier than scheduled so he'd have time to relax. He hoped she was feeling a little the same way -- about him.

The concert hall was almost filled. The first performer got through and came back on stage for her bows. Then Lilli Lehmann and her accompanist stepped out and she sang a 'specially fine group of German songs. Last, after the singer's bravos all quieted down, Rose came on stage in her 'hoop-less' gown; her upswept hair was secured with pink roses -- a dream in loveliness. She bowed gracefully and took her seat at the keyboard. The Bach went off without a hitch -- she felt good about it. Now her own composition was to be played publicly for the first time. The program notes read: *"Tintagel Rhapsody, based on a northern shore in southwest England. It was the birthplace of King Arthur of the sixth-century. Each movement deals with a phase in the life of the unhappy King, ending in a hymn-like melody depicting Queen Guinevere's exile to a nunnery, each character suffering because of an ill-guided dart from Cupid's bow."*

When Rose's last note ceased vibrating there was a standing ovation and clamor for more! Afterwards there was a reception and Rose got to speak to Fritz. There was a sad longing in his eyes as he took her hand. "I must see you very soon." Mr. and Mrs. Edleigh joined the two and exchanged remembrances of their first trip to Germany over a year ago. "Fritz, you must come with us tomorrow, if your schedule permits, for a tour of your city."

"That would be most delightful, Mrs. Edleigh" -- with such formality that Carnelia expected him to click his heels together and salute German-fashion. "What time shall we pick you up... and your address," asked Carnelia.

"I live with a family on Unter den Linden, Number 12. I am free after the noon hour," said he -- glancing over to Rose with a question in his eyes.

"Fritz, my mother brought her violin, maybe she will join us in a musical at my quarters... she is quite an exceptional player. I will engage the drawing room for any evening you are free."

"That would be marvelous," as he eased up on his stiff manner, "until tomorrow at noon then. Good evening."

Rose became something of a star overnight; the Sunday papers had a review of the performance with much emphasis on the young English composer. Herr Tausig was proud of her -- that's what counted.

"Your young friend seems to be most anxious to please, Rose," said Carnelia when they let her off at her place, "we will be here on a week's holiday -- but do not want to interrupt your study schedule. If you can work it in, we would like to have you go to Wittenberg; it would take an entire day, but it would mean so much to have you with us."

"I will work something out with Tausig," answered

Rose, "it is important for me to learn all I can about Germany."

They parted; the Edleighs' to their hotel. "Well, what do you think of our daughter," asked John, "isn't she lovely and accomplished? I owe it all to you, my darling 'Neelie'. There is something that bothers me though... I can't bring myself to put it in words."

"I know what it is: you are frightened. A woman can discern these things. You saw the deep attachment between Rose and Fritz. They don't know it yet themselves, but they are very much in love."

"I don't like it, Carnelia, -- there's something in the air that doesn't sit well. There is much talk at the Exchange about this Bismarck. He is turning into a despot. We've seen his rise in power, from a member of the German Diet in 1851: Ambassador to the French; Minister of Foreign Affairs; President of the Cabinet by '62; his ambition toward establishment of Prussia as head of the German Nation; his annexation of Schleswig-Holstein two years later; then the defeat of the Austrians last year. There are murmurings of a Franco-German War. If it just wasn't for Rose's happiness over her music progress with Herr Tausig -- we'd all go home -- the sooner the better!"

The next morning there was a messenger at Rose's residence. It was sent along with a news clipping about the debut of a young English composer at the Concert Hall. Rose was dizzy from all the accolade -- then she read the note from her teacher saying that Franz Liszt would like to hear more about this budding composer; "Could they meet at Herr Tausig's studio?"

"Yes", said Rose... "I am almost finished with 'Un Sospiro'... and perhaps he would play it for me."

When the Edleighs stopped by for Rose, she

showed them the news items and note. Mother and father both had decided to tell Rose before the week was out that they thought it best for her to return to London -- but now they looked at each other in great consternation. How could they tear down her castles? They would wait and see. The driver of the hansom (that's what they called these two-wheeled carriages with the driver sitting at an elevation) was given Fritz's address. What a splendid street -- a great avenue of stately trees, embassies, and the Royal Palace. Fritz was awaiting them, and coming toward them. Rose sprang out of the conveyance hollering, "Guten Tag, Fritz, wie geht es Ihnen?"

The parents expected him to jump up on the seat with the driver -- but no such thought occurred to Rose or him. Everything was still crystallized in sparkling ice -- but the wind had calmed down. They just all crowded in together. Under the lap blanket Fritz felt for Rose's hand and Mrs. Edleigh patted it and jumped when she saw her husband take out his pipe to light. Two faces turned red! -- but were not noticed by father or daughter, who began smoothing her blowing hair.

Fritz thought they would enjoy seeing the American-designed Benjamin Franklin Kongress Halle with the monumental staircase that descended to a reflecting pool; then the Hochschule für Musik. After that the Charlottenburg Castle would finish off their day. He explained that construction began on it in 1695; Sophie Charlotte, the first queen of Prussia, chose the site. In front of it stood the equestrian monument built to the Great Elector in 1700. The first floor was decorated in baroque style. In the rear of the castle they saw a mausoleum constructed in 1800 as a burial place for King Frederick William III and others of the Hohenzollern clan. Some day later they might return for a walk through the delightful park and promenades around the lake. (And Fritz thought to himself... without a chaperon!... as he stole a glance at Rose.) After settling on a time for a musical soirée, they parted for their own residences... until Wednesday evening.

John, Carnelia, and Rose spent the next day just browsing and shopping in the smart shops. This was the day Father had thought to bring up the subject of Rose's future. Stopping for lunch at a sidewalk café, Mr. Edleigh addressed Rose, "My dear, you're twenty-three years old -- are you satisfied with what you are undertaking, or are you being coerced by hungry musicians? Not that we don't think you're the finest pianist we have ever heard... no flattering, dear... but we want you to be sure. Are you not lonely here -- will you be depriving yourself of a future with family and loved ones surrounding you?"

"Enough, Father, I'm going to speak plain -- I didn't realize it for a long time, but I love Fritz. He doesn't know it -- I couldn't bear to be parted from my music *and* him. You want me to come back to London, don't you? Please, Papa (just like when she was a little girl), can I stay longer?"

Carnelia looked at John with sympathy. She could feel his agony... the turmoil going on within him: his longing for a houseful of grandchildren; the splashing in the lake; the dogs barking in ecstasy; teaching them to ride the great horses he'd collected. A silence fell over the three and hung around them like a dark cloud until Rose blurted out, "Is it because Fritz is German? Our Queen Victoria's nine children all married foreigners -- most of them German."

"But we're not *royalty*," said he, "marriages were

arranged for them by Kings and Queens for political reasons. And all were not happy situations either."

"Well, here's our waiter -- let us eat and forget the matter for the time being; besides, I don't even know if Fritz cares for me -- I think we are just good friends -- and I am only day-dreaming." But mother and father knew better, so they let it drop there.

Rose spoke to her landlady about the use of the music room for Wednesday and found it was free. Carnelia with the violin, Fritz on the oboe and the clarinetist, Robert, gathered round the piano; Robert had a score of the new Gounod opera themes from *Romeo and Juliet* that had just been produced on stage in Paris this year. The four tried to follow with only the one copy on the piano rack. They were botching it up, but they could synchronize enough to tell that the love music was very beautiful. Fritz said that he would copy parts for the oboe and clarinet and Rose and Carnelia could use the original score when he finished. Then they settled themselves to start on the "Celebrated Canon" of Pachelbel. It wasn't well known, though it had been written centuries ago. They created different variations on the numerous themes, and the spirited tune aroused Mr. Edleigh from behind his paper to exclaim how delightful it was. They would use it to play for Tausig, then. Carnelia suggested following it with Schubert's "Ave Maria." So, before they realized it, the evening had slipped away. Fritz lingered long enough to speak to Rose -- he *had* to see her. "Leave early to go to Herr Tausig and I will meet you at the corner," and pressed her hand.

The Edleighs decided that since Rose showed so little interest in their going to Wittenberg, they would just go on alone. That made Rose's plans much easier,

-- as she didn't have to make up an alibi for her tryst with Fritz; they'd have an hour alone. He was awaiting her at the corner café near her teacher's place. When he saw her coming he leaped to meet her. Without thinking they both clung to each other in deepest emotion. "Rose, you love me, don't you?"

"Yes, I do." Then he said, "Something is galling me to death. My Mother has demanded that I return to Nürnberg. She has my entire life planned for me: I am supposed to wed the plump, nice Elsa whose father is going to 'fit' me into his construction business as an architect. I answered her in bitterness that I had plans of my own to finish my degree here, and secure a position in Berlin. Immediately she replied that I do as they say or they curtail my stipend. It seems they desire my future in return for the allowance they provided me."

"Oh, Fritz, they *are* your *parents*! I know how tortured you are. Could you not find a job as translator for visiting dignitaries -- your English is so good. Perhaps Father could speak a word for you at the Royal Exchange in London, since they have negotiations in Berlin constantly." ...Then a hush fell over the two as they gazed at each other -- and in that silence the young people knew that this was a reality of life.

"My darling," Rose spoke, "I faced almost the same session with my father. He excuses his desire for me to return to England on the unrest in German politics. He is fearful that Bismarck is out to swallow up France and that I'll get caught abroad."

Nothing got settled, for it was time for her lesson, and Franz Liszt would be there, as he was in the city for a concert at the Hochschule für Musik. Her professor requested her playing first the "Rhapsody" that she had written. When she finished the piece Herr Liszt only sat there, gazing out the window without a word -- seconds passed like hours. She felt foolish; how could she have been deceived by her teacher into thinking she had accomplished something that should be heard by the greatest of all musicians!... "Sir, I apologize for presuming on your time and interest, please forgive me for my conceit." And she started to move from the piano. Liszt arose and putting out his hand to restrain her, said in his poor broken English, "It was from your heart, young lady -- you show too much of yourself. How do I say it in English... be more sub -- subtle.... Technique, yes -- very bravissimo!" and turning to Karl, he spoke in German -- (she couldn't catch much, but she distinctly heard him say, '"*Es gefällt mir.*")

Tausig asked him if she might play the "Un Sospiro" ...

"Ach, indeed!" -- afterwards she clearly understood his 'Bravo'... "So you would steal my own dust!" (She wondered how on earth he picked up that idiom.)

Liszt stood up to go... and kissing both her hands he left. Karl Tausig's chest swelled with pride. "I am pleased with you, Rose. Vot's troubling you, leibling?"

"I shall bring Fritz next lesson and let him explain it better to you. Thank you, Maestro," and she took leave.

John and Carnelia had not returned from Wittenberg, so she crawled beneath the covers to study her German vocabulary.

CHAPTER 6

*Back to a small town on the Alabama
River, U.S.A.... Late 1920's.*

Wendy had not put the writing down since she reached home from her piano lesson. It was almost supper time. "Wendy, have you studied your Latin lesson yet? You know exams come up real soon," said Mama from the kitchen.

She decided to take the 'bull by the horns' (what on earth does that really mean, thought she), and entered the dining room while stating, "Mama, I'm not going to pass Latin -- there's no way I can make a 65 on my exam -- and that's what I need to skim by."

"Uh huh, so you go to summer school all summer instead of Burnt Corn!"... At the thought of another season at *that place*... well, summer school didn't seem so bad. "How about signing me up at Colonel Dinkin's Academy ahead of time? If I'm this bad in Latin *this* year how could I do third semester next year!" It made sense -- and Mama had already learned it didn't help to threaten cessation of piano lessons. She might as well have *something* to excel in, her mother reasoned.

Wendy got to liking the idea of going through Live Oak Cemetery every morning -- in the cool shade of the two-hundred-year-old trees and stopping to chat at Miss Edleigh's grave. She could talk to her about wanting to be a concert pianist without anybody laughing at her. The Academy was just on the other side of the exit gate. There were tales about the Colonel's idiosyncrasies -- but she didn't mind. She'd just have longer to practice and some good excuses for shirking some of the household chores -- what with all that studying she'd have to do. The Colonel, they said, used a big long cane which he rapped on the desk for class to come to order -- and the same one on the backsides of those who didn't.

Exams came -- sure 'nuff she didn't make but 55. Oh well, she'd start all over and study each assignment every single day -- next year would be easy then. The third of June Eekie left to go to her aunt's for the summer. So now Josephine was the only one left on the block. They swapped paper dolls... they were connoisseurs, just collectors. Jo sold Wendy one of her Delineator 'boy with the grapes' for thirty of her Sears Roebuck ones. It was at her house that she had a Co-ca-Cola for the first time.

"Gosh, I hate it!" and gagged. The phone rang. Of course it was Mama saying time to get started on the Latin! *Amo, amas, amat, amamos, amais, amant.* All of a sudden it dawned on her. Those old Romans said two or three words in one. That's what those different endings meant: I love, you love, he, she, it loves... then the plural: we love, you love, they love. Where had she been all this time!

Life took on a new meaning... The Colonel wasn't so bad. Sometimes he'd leave the room, one of the boys would set the clock up a few minutes. He quickly returned, walked straight to the culprit's desk, pulled him up by the ear and whacked his rear with the cane. It was a long time before they learned he wasn't a wizard, but she went in his office one day and found out he could see a reflection of the classroom in the glass frame of a portrait of George Washington that hung on the wall.

The summer fled -- Wendy's music developed. She was proficient at Mozart, and her teacher wanted her to enter the piano contest to be held in Montgomery. There was a "Bach Invention" and the "Scotch Poem" by MacDowell that was 'required playing'. The third was the contestant's choice and she selected Paderewski's "Minuet l'Antique." No one was more amazed at the announcement of the winner than Wendy... she came in first place. Naturally, Mama and Papa were proud -- but they still nagged about school work. "You cannot enter a Conservatory without finishing High School -- so it's up to you, my girl!"

She had a math teacher who loved good music; he took special pains with her and she did O.K. But for the rest of her life, she'd remember Caesar's Conquests; it started out "Gallia est omnis divisa in partis, tris quarum unam incolunt Belgae"... etc. Sometimes she wished Caesar had not made that conquest into Gaul! English composition was her best subject; in an essay she could say what she thought -- just so it was punctuated and spelled correctly.

Eighth grade was more grown-up. Wilbur, next-door, had gone on to High School, so she didn't have to see him much any more. Soon it would be Halloween -- a night she'd never forget. Some older boys and girls dared one of their group to spend the night on a tombstone at the cemetery. This girl was the kind that would do anything to be the center of interest. She went to the Indian Princess' grave and, just for precaution, took a large butcher knife with her. The grave was only a grassy mound framed-in with low iron grill-work edging. Having lain down, she plunged the knife into the ground close by her side. Everything was un-eventful 'til around midnight... then she heard a move-ment in the dark. It grew closer and closer. Fright-ened, she decided to get up but something grabbed at her skirt -- she couldn't get free. Later in the wee hours one of the 'darers' went to see if she was fudging on them. She was dead. The doctor said it was her weak heart. The knife had plunged through her heavy skirt and pinned her down.

This was the last year of Latin -- and it looked like she was going to get a high C+ average in it. Ninth grade found Wendy a 'big knot on a little log', as the jargon went. These were depression years and any little change picked up by odd jobs went into the bank for college. She helped a local organ-tuner with his work, and sometimes played for the dancing school, as long as it left enough time for practice and homework.

Wendy was not forgetting the yellowed manu-script that lay in her bureau drawer -- so as it was Thanksgiving holidays, she took it out and started read-ing where she'd left off.

CHAPTER 7

In Berlin 1870

The Edleighs returned from Wittenberg too late that night to see their daughter. They had two more days in Berlin before returning home. Sending a message to Rose by a courier, they suggested the three lunch at the Tiergarten together. She hastily wrote a reply to be sent by the errand boy that she would be happy to be picked up around noon, but must return by three p.m. for her German class. Rose remembered her last time at the Tiergarten with Fritz and his parents. Perhaps this would be a nicer occasion.

Upon entering the Tiergarten, one could immediately feel that this was the pride of Germany... the great 630 acre park... the equal of London's Hyde Park, or the Bois de Boulogne in France. The trees were magnificent, but the winter scenery could not compare with the gorgeous rose gardens and various flowers of the summer season that Rose described to her parents. "Then you've been here before, dear?" "Yes," she replied, "I came when Fritz's parents visited him." "Oh," and with that her voice began to break, "Fritz is in trouble with his family. They want him to return to Nürnberg where they have 'cooked up' a marriage deal with the daughter of Mr. Rhinhardt's contractor-friend. She's ugly and Fritz can't stand her -- mostly because of their devious scheming -- he hardly knows her except

69

from school days... I hate them!"

Mr. Edleigh broke in, clearing his throat, "Is that how you feel about us wanting you to come back to London? We have no such ideas of matching you up with anyone -- naturally, I hope the right fellow for you will turn up... sooner or later... when you come back to your own country."

"The right one has already 'turned up', Father... I might as well tell you, Fritz and I love each other. He is defying his parents, giving up his allowance from them in order to stay on in Berlin."

"What will he do for his expenses? Can he obtain part-time work or an apprenticeship with an architect until he finishes his degree?"

"That's what I want to talk to you about, Papa." (Oh, oh. So she's a little girl again, smiled Mr. Edleigh to himself.) "Could you recommend him as a translator to your business friends when they come to Berlin?"

"My darling Daughter, what I've been trying to warn you about is the future of England's business with Germany -- Bismarck is dangerous. He has us all trembling!"

Carnelia had recommended *casseler rippspeer*, a concoction of salted pork fried to a golden crisp in butter -- then slowly cooked until done. This was the 'house specialty.' With that there would be fresh asparagus, cabbage and a mug of beer. When it arrived at the table, all were too glum to eat heartily. Besides Rose hated beer! *"Nein bier, kaffee bitte,"* Rose said to the waiter, proudly showing off her learning to them. They ate a quiet lunch. Rose jumped up quickly, and looking at her watch stated, *"Viertel nach zwei* -- I'll be late." So they asked for a cab and left, seeing little of the marvelous park... and settling no issues about the future.

"Tonight, Rose -- we'll pick you up at your residence around 6:30. We will dine at our hotel and talk more," as her father pecked a kiss on her forehead. At dinner at the expensive hotel, Mr. Edleigh tried to lighten the tension by telling Rose about their excursion to Wittenberg. "Do you know much about Martin Luther? He is the main reason we do not attend Catholic services, but belong to the Church of England -- at least one of the reasons; 'course Henry VIII really decided that for the British when he defied the Pope by marrying Anne Boleyn -- but you know all that. Probably there wouldn't have been a Protestant church had it not been for Luther. I won't go into details, but Luther did some defying when he nailed his *Ninety-five Theses* on the main door of the Castle Church of Wittenberg in 1517. Here, Rose, I copied this from a plaque that was preserved under glass. Luther prefixed his proclamation with this:

> **Out of the love for the faith and the desire to bring it to light, the following propositions will be discussed at Wittenberg under the chairmanship of the Reverend Father Martin Luther, master of Arts and Sacred Theology and Lecturer in Ordinary on the same at that place. Wherefore he requests that those who are unable to be present and debate orally with us may do so by letter.**

"It all started over money, you know. Tertzel had questioned the Pope, 'why not sell indulgences for the souls in Purgatory, and release them sooner, and with the money from the transactions of the buyers build a splendid church?'

"Oh, Rose, I wish you had been with us -- the city itself is so interesting. Well, you have years ahead of you yet," said Carnelia. "Not if Father has his way" -- and she shot an accusing look at him -- "he wants to whisk me away before I get a chance to see any of the old towns and scenery!"

"Rose, if you feel that way we will lengthen our holiday and take you to Nürnberg -- perhaps you would like Fritz to come along." Rose jumped up and hugged her father with affection -- "Oh, I'd love that. I'm certain Herr Tausig will understand. He hasn't been well lately; ... you know, he is only three years older than I am and he looks so tired. (Little did she think that in two years he would be dead... and just barely thirty.) When do we go, and where *all* do we go?".

"Don't you think you better approach your friend first, and see how it is with him?" said Carnelia. The remainder of the evening went joyfully. Rose made a point of contacting Fritz on the next day with the invitation. He couldn't take his eyes off her face, hair, beautiful hands (she had finally grown to them -- but she'd never forget Cook's telling about her 'ugly extremities') -- he wanted to hold her close -- but conventions didn't permit. "Fritz, my parents are stretching their visit and they want me to see more of Germany -- especially Nürnberg since Richard Wagner's *Die Miestersinger* will be produced at Munich this year... and there is the St. Sebaldus Cathedral at Nürnberg of the 14th century. I'll bet you have already studied the

architecture of its interior. Forgive me for going on so.
They want you to come with us. Please find a way."

"Darling, I don't think my parents would receive
me at this time."

"But you don't have to stay with them. We will
take a suite of rooms, and you can be our guide," Rose
interrupted. "Father will hire a large hansom cab for
all of us -- you and he can take turns driving. Wouldn't
it be great!"

"I'll go, Rose, but my funds are low, so you must
let me pull my own weight by doing the driving, han-
dling the luggage and translating. When are you planning to leave? It will take three hard days' traveling to
cover the distance... but there's much to see along the
way."

To heck with conventions! Rose threw her arms
around Fritz. He would be ready the following day.
This was the most impromptu trip Carnelia had ever
heard of. Things were thrown into the valises... transportation was arranged by Mr. Edleigh and, after picking up Fritz, away they flew. Their route would take
them through Teltow, where they stopped to rest the
horses and eat the lunch that Rose and Carnelia had
prepared.   They must quit before they reached
Blakenfelde for the night. An early start in the morning would permit them to reach Treuenbrietzen by
nightfall; then the third day they could go more leisurely and arrive at dusk in Nürnberg.

Fritz suggested he stop at his parent's home before going any farther. He rang the front bell and his
father answered the summons. When he saw who it
was... and the other three English persons he slammed
the door in his son's face! Fritz knew no words would
help: that they had made up their minds to disinherit

him. Walking sadly toward his companions, Rose ran
out to take his arm. Everybody was tired so they settled at a zimmer -- they needed three rooms. After a
night's sleep they'd feel more like sightseeing. The
Edleighs were so sorry for Fritz and his parents being
estranged; it cast a pall over them all... but he had
made a choice, now he must accept it. Time would
lessen the pain.

Nürnberg was much larger than they expected --
with a population of close to a half million. It dated
back to the mid-eleventh century. Everywhere they
looked handicrafts caught their eye. Fritz told them
that Richard Wagner had not invented the Mastersingers or Minnesingers --- that Tannhauser was a real
citizen of the 13th century, and their most famous citizen was Hans Sachs, a shoemaker and poet. He was
from here and died here. Germany's greatest painter
was Albrecht Dürer, a native -- and there were others:
Veit Stoss, one of the greatest woodcarvers; and Adam
Kraft, Germany's finest carvers in stone. Among Nürnberg's inventions were the gunlock, mechanical toys,
pocket watches and the first geographical globe.

Nürnberg was situated in beautiful natural parks
and forests. They would have their lunch in the Volks-
park Dutzendreich where there were several beautiful
ponds. The Pegnitz River separated the town, making
it like twin cities -- each with its surrounding wall.
Rose was intrigued with the 12th century Kaiserburg
(the Imperial Castle) with its Imperial Hall, and the
Renaissance double-chapel. In the courtyard was a
165-foot well and a round tower that offered wonderful
views of the city. Rose laughed when she saw Gan-
semännchenbrunnen (Gooseman's Fountain), she didn't
know which was the whackiest: the name of the thing

or the bronze figure of the old peasant taking two geese to the market. She always had a soft spot for the under-dog -- or should she say under-geese, poor things -- but maybe they were just going for a walk! That was a particular Rose-reaction; one minute a serious concert artist, the next a little mischievous kid. That's why everyone loved her -- 'cept Mrs. Rhinhardt!

They went to see the eleventh-century St. Matha Church where the Mastersingers had a singing school from 1578 to 1620.

By now the four were exhausted and returned to the zimmer. Rose and Fritz had a brief time together alone. Fritz was about to crack-up: his frustration over his parents' treatment and his imminent future was too much. "Rose, I think I'll join up with Bismarck's troops and cool my heels awhile."

"Do you mean you want to stop seeing me any-more?" said Rose, with tears welling up in her eyes.

"It's not that -- it's that it all seems so hopeless with me for the while being."

Rose replied, "Then I'll make my family happy by returning to England. We can write -- and when you've 'cooled-off' enough we can make decisions," responded Rose.

To Rose Edleigh, Prince Otto Eduard Leopold von Bismarck was just a bullish beast that wanted to take over all Europe. Another Napoleon, but more cunning. He wasn't called the "Iron Chancellor" for nothing! He was bent on the establishment of Prussia as the head of a great German nation. When the lower house would not pass his budget and bills he just simply dissolved the Diet... and upon the German people be-coming nervous and excited over it, he merely diverted their attention by a controversy with Denmark which resulted in annexation of Schleswig-Holstein in 1864. That was followed by defeating Austria in 1866 -- and now this business of taking over France. And *this* was who Fritz wanted to join up with! From where she stood, the results of Bismarck's success as a capable statesman in the future didn't matter, he was the monster standing between herself and Fritz.

They would leave Nürnberg the next morning. Fritz sent a message to his mother; he simply couldn't leave with her thinking him a thankless son. "Mother, I love you and Father. No matter what the future holds I know I could never be happy with your plans for my life. I hope to return to your good graces someday. Your son, Fritz."

The trip back to Berlin was miserable for the young two. Carnelia and John kept pointing out the marvelous scenery and the ancient castles, but Rose couldn't see them through her misty eyes.

Upon returning to Berlin, matters were soon set into motion. Mr. and Mrs. Edleigh went to Professor Tausig's for Rose's last lesson... they asked Fritz to go and interpret for them. Karl Tausig spoke freely about Rose's possibility of becoming a concert pianist in a short time -- perhaps within the next two years. "If you feel that she should leave Berlin, then I can recommend her to a fine colleague of mine, Arthur Sullivan, much respected in your London. He will be a great help with Rose in composition. It always benefits to have someone who can introduce you to the musical sphere -- and who can promote public appearances."

"Yes, we have heard of Arthur Sullivan. We read in the *London Times* that he and Gilbert, a librettist, had begun a partnership and three of their operas were to be played this year," said Rose's father.

"I have the good fortune of having some courtesy tickets for *Die Meistersinger* for tonight's performance if you can use them."

"Oh, yes," exclaimed Rose... "you can come, can't you Fritz?" He could.

On the way back they stopped for a light supper on which Fritz splurged almost the last of his waning capital. It didn't matter, though, for tomorrow he'd be leaving Berlin to join the German Army. Rose was in no mood for comic opera, but it provided her and Fritz a chance to hold each other's hand in the darkness of the auditorium. They wrote notes to one another on the back of the libretto -- swearing their eternal love. He would see her on his first furlough... even if he had to go to London.

It would take a few days to organize Rose's belongings, make travel plans, and pack. The new cable had been perfected, leading between all important transoceanic countries, so John Edleigh thought he would reach London in short notice so that the stable could make their preparations to meet them at Victoria Station. There were too many bundles to manage the trains out to Hampstead Heath.

CHAPTER 8

Hampstead Heath

Christmas came and passed. By the first of February, they had made arrangements for Rose to begin lessons with Arthur Sullivan. He was amazed at her technical ability and interpretations. She played a Chopin Nocturne for him and was complimented on the phrasing of a certain passage. "You know, Miss Edleigh, when one misphrases a melody, it's like reading a part in a foreign language and putting the accent on the incorrect syllable, so that you do not understand it nor does the native in whose tongue you try to be understood. Now, let me hear some of your own compositions that Tausig wrote me so much about."

Rose chose her "Toccato in F minor"... a contrapuntal piece. Sullivan was astounded at the maturity of her style. Her scale work was so crystal clear... like a string of pearls, each cascading over a smooth surface. "I will certainly be expecting you to play at the young artist's concert in the Crystal Palace in two weeks -- Queen Victoria generally appears at these performances. I understand from your last teacher that you have played for Franz Liszt; that is a marvelous experience that you must cherish."

The first session went smoothly -- but what an assignment to prepare in a week's time! She was relieved, however, to have something to keep her mind off Fritz. The train took her out to Hampstead and she walked the three blocks home. Carnelia ran out to greet her, waving a letter in her hand from Germany! Rose tried to look calm but it was all she could do to keep from snatching the precious parcel from her. "How did you like your new professor, dear?" "Fine, but he's not much older than I am... Please forgive me, but I've got to be alone a moment."

She tore open the envelope and began to read:
My darling Rose,

I miss you so -- if your image was not before my eyes constantly, I could not go on! I was told that the first three weeks were the hardest: -- if I survive it, it will be because I've become hardened to it. I am confused and miserable. If I am commanded to do this... it's immediately rescinded, and I'm told to do something different! We drill and drill and drill 'til I want to tear the drill master's throat out.

Yesterday, I spent the day at the infirmary -- I think they are using us as candidates for some kind of vaccine experiments. I'm so afraid when I leave my quarters that I might forget protocol when I meet an officer, that I find myself saluting my own bunk-house fellows. One thing I've learned: keep my mouth shut! Joking doesn't go far here.

Enough of that. How is your new piano professor working out? Do you like him? Oh, if I could just see you. I don't know from one day to another where we will be. So it will be difficult for you to write. But our love will survive... keep holding on to that.

Your own Fritz

Rose's eyes were brimming over with tears. She couldn't join the family yet. In all situations when she felt helpless she had learned from Nanny to ask the Lord to take over the matter... and afterwards she felt the tension leave her. Now she went down to the drawing room for tea. She found Mr. and Mrs. George du Maurier with her parents. Rose liked Emma Wightwick du Maurier, an English lady who had tried hard to break some of George's bad Parisian ways: admiring pretty faces, smoking too many cigarettes, and sometimes getting a bit too tipsy. "But after all," she whispered to Carnelia, "he is said to be the illegitimate grandson of the Duke of York and Mary Anne Clarke - - sh-sh --."

George du Maurier just radiated with a sort of warmth that drew everyone to him... a man with no enemies. He strode over to the piano and said to Rose, "Shall we have some music?"

"May I join in", asked Carnelia, and they selected a tenor song of Alfredo from *La Traviata*, by Verdi. It was the version based on Dumas's *Camille*. After that, Schubert's "Ave Maria" was requested. Carnelia's violin playing was as good as ever. Soon dusk overtook them and the guests thought it proper to leave... but with the promise of many more delightful musicales.

Early the next morning, Rose lit in on her piano assignment, working until noon; then dug out the German text book to continue her study... someday maybe she could talk with Fritz in his own tongue. The days continued in this manner until the scheduled day for

80

the program at the Crystal Palace. She wore the lovely dress that Carnelia had sent her in Berlin. Her father and mother were proud to accompany her in the hansom cab they had hired.

Even though arriving early, it seemed like all London had thought of the same thing. Father escorted Rose around to the back of the stage then joined his wife. There were four young musicians on the program. One was a violinist, another a soprano, and two were pianists. Rose parted the curtain on the stage and took a peek at the attendance. The Queen she spotted first, flanked on one side by Mr. Disraeli and on the other by John Brown. Brown had been her almost constant companion after she came out of her painful mourning for her beloved Albert's death. Brown had been excellent with the horses and had prevented several accidents while the Queen was riding at Balmoral Castle -- (in fact, he was her constant protector, accompanying her to Germany, taking charge of her pony carriage in 1864).

As the Queen took her seat in the Royal stall, the entire audience stood and applauded for several minutes. Then the curtain rose and Mr. Arthur Sullivan introduced the four musicians. After they retired from the stage, the pianist from Bournemouth played his group: a Liszt number and Thalbert's "Variations on a Palestrina Theme;" following that, the soprano sang an aria from Mozart's *Don Giovanni*, the violinist did some lesser work of Leopold Mozart (father of Wolfgang A. Mozart); then Rose came to the piano and bowed deeply to the Queen, who stood in response to her compliment -- the entire audience arose in a body and faced Victoria. When all was calm, she sat at the keyboard and her heart said, "I dedicate this music to you,

my dearest Fritz."   Her nimble fingers played the
"Toccato" flawlessly; and without much pause, she went

into the Chopin "Nocturne in B," a luxuriant melody, but with a morbid lyricism in the second part... returning to its appealing warmth in the end. Sullivan thought he had never heard it played so well.

There was an uproar after her performance. She blushed at the curtain calls for "Rose... Rose... Rose!"

Her debut into the concert world had been made. The Queen sent her a note of appreciation, asking her to Buckingham Palace for a State function.

"Well, dear, you made quite a splash tonight; we're so proud of you, Rose," said her father... and Carnelia gave her a squeeze. The Edleighs decided to take a flat in the city. His business demanded more commuting into London these days, and too, Rose would be nearer her teacher. Weekends could be in Hampstead. they would take two servants with them. Nobody could prepare food like Cook... and the house-keeper was used to their ways.

After the house-searching was completed, they lost no time getting settled in the Kensington area, not far from Hyde Park. It would be close to everything. One of the horses would be brought and stabled close by for Rose to ride in Rotten Row -- upon hearing it called that, she laughed. It seemed very fresh to her!

There was no way to let Fritz know about the London address, but he had the Hampstead one, so she would have to wait it out 'til they returned to Hampstead on various weekends. But each time there would be nothing amongst the accumulated mail. Only music could soothe her heart-sickness, and she would have practiced all day if Carnelia hadn't made up excursions or shopping trips or tea at the Savoy. Somehow winter passed... and spring... and summer! No word from Germany. "Carnelia, something has gone wrong... I know it has."

That night Father came bungling in the front door. What on earth! Has he been chased by a beast? The housekeeper opened up and there stood the largest dog she'd ever seen, with a leash attached to her employer, "Why, my soul, Sir, where did the mutt find you!"

"It's not a 'mutt', it's a St. Bernard. I couldn't resist him -- with his looking so much like old Barnabus." Rose ran to greet them and immediately the dog took to her, slobbering all over her skirt. "Father, what on earth -- how can we keep him in this city flat?"

"We'll take him out to Hampstead," replied he. In the next five minutes, serious doubts about their recent acquisition arose. That beautiful Ming jar that Carnelia had just over-bid on at the antique auction sat resplendently on the tea table that lay in the path of Barnabus and his intended destination and wham!... "Sweep it up, quick, before Carnelia returns -- maybe she'll not notice its absence until after she's fallen in love with Mr. 'B'," yelled John Edleigh. "Give him some food and show him his hang-out and maybe it will cool him down."

Upon returning, Carnelia was aware of something missing... she also smelled a different aroma in the air. "Uh, huh," as she spied the vacated spot on the table. "Where is it -- and what did you do with *him*?" trying to look like Napoleon in his stance... one hand on her chest and the other behind her back, giving each one 'the eye'.

At that instant the kitchen door burst open and Barnabus ran to her side, licking her hands and welcoming her to his new home! Carnelia melted and grabbed the brute in her arms.

"We'll take him out to Hampstead tomorrow," John promised.

"Darling, he is so wonderful," said Carnelia, forgetting the precious broken antique. At noon Friday they packed for a weekend at Hampstead. The stableman had come with the coach to take the luggage, two maids, the Edleighs -- and Barnabus -- home. First thing off, Rose searched the mail box. Empty! "Don't worry, Miss Rose, there's a letter for you in the house."

There was a German postmark on the envelope.

My dearest darling Rose,

It's the first chance I've had to write. I hope you are loving me... sometimes I can hear in my mind your playing and thinking of me. I have much to tell you and so little time for that. Things are getting hot; through some fainaiguing, Bismarck has made it look like the French are declaring war on Prussia (It's really the other way around, of course. But *my* country, right or wrong.) The news is: rumor got out and found its way to the top that I spoke very good English -- and also another mate in my outfit. So we were sent to the front office to do translations and interpretations. I will be moving on tomorrow with one of the Generals. Will write you from wherever.

All of me, Fritz

Rose went to her room to be all alone, lamenting she did not even have a picture of him.

Barnabus made his way around in short order.

He thought the balls that they played croquet with were
for him to chase... and he would faithfully retrieve them
to the player. "Oh, Barn, we'll have to put you out in
the stable if we are to have our game."

Saturday morning Rose got in two hours of practice, so she was free for the rest of the weekend. She
rode old Trace, her horse since she was fourteen; he
must have been about twelve years old now. Carnelia
joined her and they rode over to Kenwood House,
surrounded by it's beautiful park and lake. There they
dismounted and sat on the grass to talk. "Carnelia, you
know I must have wondered why I've never had a little
brother or sister -- I know how you and Father love
each other. If you don't want to discuss it, it's all right."

"But I do, honey, and you should know; John and
I fell in love through our love in common for you.
When he asked if I'd marry him, I told him that I could
not bear a child and he said that was the least of his
worries. So we've been so happy just sharing our 'little
Rose.' But it brings me to my concern for you. You
should be meeting young men and have your own little
family round you. I have watched young men turning
their heads to follow you -- you're a beautiful woman
and could make any match you liked."

Rose was silent... They both acted like they were
absorbed in the delightful scenery about them. "Carnelia, I can think of no one but Fritz. He seems to be
moving up to safer quarters."

"We will talk again. John must be home now
from the Spaniards" (an old site described in books as a
once wild place where the lone man traveled warily --
as this was the retreat of highwaymen who awaited the
unsuspecting victim. But in the seventeenth century, it
was turned into a respectable Inn... now a pub).

So they mounted and rode back to the stables. John was glad that they were using the horses; they needed the airing. At supper that night he started discussing the Franco-Prussian situation. Rose listened intently. The Germans had advanced into France, captured one French army inside the fortress of Metz. At Sedan they did the same, and there Napoleon III, himself, was captured. Germany had kept hammering away, and now making a siege on Paris. There's an account on the front page that a British diplomat wrote in his column of the *London Times* that the New Germany 'looms out like some huge irontank from which no sounds are heard but the tramp, tramp, tramp of men at drill -- and carrying their monster guns.' Bismarck is determined on turning to the West. He would like to put a Hohenzollern King in Spain; they wanted a German outpost in the rear of France beyond the Pyrenees range. This was too much for the French -- the effect of such a suggestion was bound to be explosive on the French. The Minister of War in Paris said he was ready! But old Bismarck put on the innocent act and declined to press the offensive candidature... Everybody relaxed; there wouldn't be a war. Then the French Ambassador requested an audience with the King of Prussia, but was evaded. Things might have ended there, but one night Bismarck (the Chancellor) was dining in Berlin with Moltke and Roon -- they were glum because it looked like there would be no war with France. But when a telegram reached Bismarck from Ems -- he deceitfully revised it for publication which was transformed into a news item to appear that the French Ambassador had been dismissed by the King of Prussia. When this reached Paris there could be no doubt of the results; the French would be depended on to react, just as the Chancellor of Prussia had planned. Now war was within their grasp and it could be blamed on France for being the instigator.

It happened in forty-eight hours. French armies sprang forward for attack. French shells went zooming overhead and *Mitrailleuses* poured in a deadly stream of bullets. Everywhere was heard 'a Berlin.'

"But I don't understand any of this," said Rose... seconded by Carnelia. "Could Fritz be somewhere in all that tumult, do you think?" asked Rose.

"Perhaps you'll get word soon... Would anyone care for some card games?" asked John. The two women were tired from their ride and declined... "maybe tomorrow night."

Sunday morning they attended services at the nearby Parish Church. The Reverend Bertram Aston was still the rector there. He kissed Rose on the forehead just as if she was still that same little girl of long ago. All through the sermon she couldn't help praying for Fritz's safety... "and if anything happened, Lord, let me be able to endure."

At the close of the last prayer, they all gathered at the front of the church commending Rose on the wonderful notices she had received in the London paper. She thanked them all in a humble manner and joined John and Carnelia to walk to their house.

Summer was about on them. Nanny's grave could be covered with roses now. It seemed to be the favorite spot that Barnabus liked to flop for a nap. The Edleighs spent more time at Hampstead since the warm weather started. Days drowsed by. Rose's teacher told her she needed to be at the Academy of Music to work on her Master's degree so that she could qualify for a position of teaching to fill in between concerts as the time went on.

She enrolled in September and could be working on her thesis until May. The courses seemed easy enough, though academics were not her forte. When Christmas came she would have a long rest out at Hampstead -- away from all this talk of war that was blaring constantly on the streets of London. In the meanwhile, she was to play Chopin's *Concerto #2* (F Minor) with the Royal Academy Orchestra. It was the melody of the second movement that always saddened her. Sullivan said she played it like her heart was breaking. "It is, Maestro. Someday I will tell you all about it, if you will let me."

"Anything that permeates your music is important to me," he assured her.

The recital would be finished a week before the holidays; that phase of the semester's work completed. Now if she could pass the exam in German class!

When she arrived at Hampstead Station the coach from the stables met her; with all her luggage she couldn't walk the distance. Going down the walkway to her home she had a funny sensation. No Barnabus leaping up on her, no Carnelia, no anything. Then her eyes fell on the silver tray that contained the mail. There was a letter from France in a strange hand. Hastily she tore into it:

Dear Rose,

This is a hard letter to write. I am William Tilly, who was a friend of Fritz. We were assigned to two Generals... as their aides, because we spoke good English. Last evening, the coach bearing General Hermann, to whom Fritz was attached, turned over on the outskirts of Metz. Fritz saved the General's life by breaking his fall on the rocks below, costing him his life... I will notify his parents, as I took his address book off his person.

He will be buried with honors. When... and if... things are ever over, I will come to England -- as I loved Fritz as a brother.

Sadly, William Tilly

Like one with a stroke... Rose sat paralyzed, her eyes fixed on the letter. She knew not what the day or hour was. This was what 'oblivion' was. Carnelia found her and immediately could see what had happened. She splashed her hands in cold water then soothed her forehead, brushing her hair back from her face. Slowly Rose turned to face her mother. She reached for her voice -- but it was gone. "You're in shock, Lovey. Can you stand? I'll get Begonia to help me carry you to your room."

"Where's Barnabus?" she finally was able to say. "He's coming, Rose." For once, sensing something amiss, he didn't jump all over the place with joy and lick at her feet. He padded behind them and jumped on the bed beside her, snuggling his head beneath her arms.

"Ah, Miss Rose, Begonia will fix you up with a nice cup of hot tea," said Cook. Carnelia knew that she had a formula for such occasions -- a brandy or something that would soothe and quieten her nerves... she had used it when her 'periods' were so bad.

Rose slept all night. John and Carnelia took turns looking in on her. She survived the worst and in about a week was able to discuss things in general with her parents. "Father, I've never known how you must have hurt when your wife died -- and here I've known Fritz only two years, and have seen him very sparingly. I suppose it was all the drama surrounding our attachment... even to the point of estrangement with his parents and joining the army. I shall write to his family immediately and let them know how sorry I am." She hoped her German was good enough to express herself... perhaps her German Professor would help her when she returned to London in January.

CHAPTER 9

- 1871 -

Rose never cared whether the Franco-Prussian War was over or not -- or who won! From now on, music was her life. Arthur Sullivan, who had become her trusted friend and teacher read to her from one of Martin Luther's tracts: "A Fair and Glorious Gift".

I wish to see all arts principally music in the service of Him who gave and created them. Music is a glorious and fair gift of God. I would not for the world forego my humble share of music. Singers are never sorrowful, but are merry, and smile through their troubles in song. Music makes people kinder, gentler, more staid and reasonable. I am strongly persuaded that after theology there is no art that can be placed on a level with music: for besides theology, music is the only art capable of affording peace and joy of the heart. The devil flees before the sound of music almost as much as before the Word of God.
Martin Luther

"But then we come to the meaning of 'Art.' What is 'Art,' Rose?" At her hesitation to define it he continued, "Art is the embodiment of noble thought. Then we come to the discernment part -- many canvases hang in the galleries; yesterday I viewed a work of Gustave Courbet, the French realist. He was present and sounding off in a lecture expressing contempt for reli-

92

gious and classical themes. He said mockingly, 'Show me an angel and I will paint one.' His canvases were almost brutal delineations. His Compatriot Honoré Daumier did lithographs that were satirical of his subjects among the political circles, the bourgeoisie and even the Courts of law. Soon that will intrude into the realm of music. So we must protect and pass down what is noble and uplifting. I judge a book to be good if the reading of it makes me strive to be a better man.

"So now, Miss Edleigh, let me hear what you have done on the Schumann number."

She sat at the keyboard just running through some scales and arpeggios to warm up -- then lit into the "Novelette."

"Excellent, my dear. What would you like to start on next? Perhaps a Chopin Etude. Of all Chopin's music the Etudes are the most demanding."

"Whatever you advise... I'm ready to work -- my life from now on *is* music!"

Upon reaching her twenty-ninth birthday, Rose had her degree from the Royal Academy of Music, London. She was in demand at the Conservatory as concert pianist and teacher. She was no stranger to Buckingham Palace, and there existed mutual admiration between herself and Queen Victoria. It was an eclectic era that bore the designation of 'Victorian Period' -- a romantic age. The drawing room set the stage and the props were bric-a-brac, whatnots, ringlets, crinolines and blushing ladies.   Morals were the Queen's business -- and she meant to see that England stayed that way. She encouraged the Tennysons, American Longfellows, or Heines -- Landseer engravings, or anyone who played Liszt well on the pianoforte. Time stalked onward.

This was the year of the opening of the Albert Hall, another memorial of the Queen's to her 'Beloved Angel.' It was built from the profits of the Great Exhibition, which Londoners many years later would have reason to bless the perpetuation of the memory of Prince Albert, Consort. The attendance at the opening of the Albert Hall and Blackfriars Bridge, both in 1871, were two of the very few public appearances the Queen made. This was also the year of much criticism of her 'neglecting her duty,' as Sir Charles Dilke put it in a public lecture given in New Castle. There formed a rift between herself and Gladstone because he did not repudiate a charge that 'she had hoards of savings stowed away for her private use.' This all brought on extreme illness to Victoria... and public sympathy soon swayed in her favor.

Rose took up her position at the Academy with enthusiasm, still studying with Sullivan to further her career. She found herself filled with genuine delight... passing on something wonderful to another person gave her a sense of responsibility and importance. The faculty was to give a concert before Christmas and she was asked to play the Chopin "Etude Opus 25 in G Flat Major." It was a favorite with everyone... called the 'Butterfly Etude'. Its rendition was so well received, that it wasn't surprising when she opened the envelope with the Queen's seal, and found a request for a command performance at the new Albert Hall.

Weekends at Hampstead were farther apart now, but when she could, she would see her parents at tea or an occasional dinner. Her father talked to her about a possible trip to America within the year, perhaps in August. He wished she might think about going with them -- and right off she thought it would be wonderful! John said, "I've never discussed it much with you, but we have relatives in America. I had a long letter from my Uncle John telling about the ending of the War over the slave question. It was called the Civil War -- but was everything *but* civil. Of course, we've had ours here, too, but not about the same thing. John Poderfoy lives in Alabama, a state down in the southern part of the United States. It was in a dangerous territory during the war (as it was the arsenal of the Confederacy) over the issue of slavery. Even though the fighting ended in 1865, things were still hard in the South and the land that used to be so fertile and rich is now hardly fit to grow potatoes -- much less the abundance of cotton that its economy was based on. Uncle John would like to see me -- I was his favorite nephew as a boy. He will make accommodations for us if we let him know when. It seems he has some business matters to talk to me about. His letter is postmarked Selma, Alabama. You think it over, Rose, and when we go to Hampstead for Christmas... perhaps by then you will have made up your mind."

"Father, one of the Professors at the Academy knows German, in fact he teaches it; he has helped me write a letter to Fritz's parents. I cannot bear to think of how they must be suffering -- and feeling guilt over taking the stand they did about his marriage; that that was what led him to join the Army -- and to his death.

I have lost all my bitterness about the past. I know
now that we all go at God's appointed time."

"Rose, my little girl has come a long, long way!
You are teaching your old father some things I should
have known many years ago."

Carnelia spoke up, "Now if I can break into the
conversation, I think we better get to the station before
the last run. We'll hug Barnabus for you. He caught a
chipmunk the other day by the tail, played with him for
a while then let him go, no worse for the capture. See
you for the Christmas holidays."

CHAPTER 10

On Sunday, the London paper had a write up about the "Melodious evening at the Crystal Palace starring a composer-pianist of rare artistry. Her flawless execution of the difficult cadenza and the *'Allegro Appassionato'* was deserving of the standing ovation she received after playing the Chopin Etude. Miss Rose Edleigh's encore was her own work entitled "A Sad Song," which depicted deep pathos without being maudlin. The world will soon know this scintillating young star."

She cut out the clipping just in case Father neglected that section of the paper, and took it with her to Hampstead. It seemed that Barnabus knew she would arrive for he was pacing back and forth in front of the house. She flopped on the lawn with the big furry hulk -- it was glorious to be home. The weather was warm for this time of the year -- in fact Rose was feeling very happy!

At dinner, she brought up the American trip. Father brightened up immediately... and stated he would make all the arrangements and obtain all the documents for traveling abroad. The Cunard Steamship Line would be consulted first thing in the morning. "The *Britannia* made her maiden voyage four years before you were born. It was considered miraculous that she crossed the Atlantic in fourteen days and eight hours. But I'm sure the record has improved over the years. We must count on being gone at least for six weeks. When does your term at the Academy start? Perhaps we better plan on leaving here earlier than August."

Carnelia got out her violin and Rose went to the piano. They did their old favorites... and John put down his *Punch* edition and closed his eyes, thinking what a fortunate man he was. Barnabus sat at his feet flapping his tail periodically without much regard for the rhythm of Dvorak's "Humoresque." So Christmas passed on wings of song, and the holidays ended with a New Year's party that the Edleighs gave for some friends and neighbors: the George du Mauriers; the Reverend Aston; the Worthingtons (new people in the next block); John Edleigh's business partner with his wife and Mr. Arthur Sullivan who brought the brilliant librettist Gilbert. What an evening of glorious music. Du Maurier's voice with its lyrical beauty enchanted everyone. Sullivan spoke to Gilbert about Rose's talent for composition, at which Gilbert responded, "You, as a pupil of Liszt, should know. Why not the three of us collaborate on a musical play?"

Before June, 1872, the performance was given at the Conservatory. "The Queen's Blue Garter" -- a little on the risqué side, (but could just sneak by Victorian standards) was presented by the Academy Choir and dance chorus, written by Gilbert, Sullivan, and Edleigh. It was never great music, but very jolly and enjoyable.

School was out again for summer break... and the Edleighs were off to America. They drove to the Southampton docks and sailed on the *Britannia* from there. The waters were calm. Rose was thrilled throughout the voyage. She wondered what to expect of New York City... should she slip a sharp knife in her handbag if they should go on the streets. The London papers had carried stories about the corrupt boss, Fernando Wood, who ruled the City in the 1850's. Boss Tweed's dictatorship covered the late '60's and early 70's until he was brought to book largely by the courage of the *New York Times* editors.

They would not be in New York long though, for they were headed for the 'deep South'. She wondered if there would be Red Indians behind trees striking out at them with poisoned arrows. But, then, all was not so serene in England either, nor on the Continent: there was the French Commune of 1871, which, after several weeks of civil war, was squashed. Then the elections in that same year in Germany -- the Catholics had elected a large bloc of their own to the Reichstag; they were supporting independence of the Church from the State and tried to stamp out divorce, liberty of conscience and secular education. This led to the controversy known as Kulturkampf (civilization struggle). Imperial Government forbade any criticism of the Government by the Clergy. They were beginning to 'pick-on' the Jesuit Order... running them out of the country. But America had her problems, too.

They docked in New York Harbor and, hiring a cabbie, they reached the Hotel Brevoert -- a famous gathering place for writers and artists. John Edleigh telegraphed a message to his uncle in Alabama saying they had safely arrived and would start the next day by rail. There had been many improvements in railroads in the last few years -- mainly the steel rail which Vanderbilt contributed to replace the old iron tracks of the *New York Central*. Another boon to the industry was the air brake adopted in 1870, making for more efficiency and safety. In the 1860's, the Pullman cars were introduced -- but still lighted with swaying kerosene lanterns. In less than a week, in spite of the jostling, jerking, and potbelly stoves, they pulled into the train station at Selma... fortunately there had been no reason to use the heating system: on the contrary, the three complained that they'd never felt such heat as this Alabama sun!

"Well, that was a blessing to the cotton grower, my dear," said John. Then he spotted Uncle John Poderfoy in the crowd that usually gathered around the station whenever the train was due -- the kids all got great amusement at watching the old 'cowcatcher' -- (designed for pushing stray cattle off the tracks). One five-year-old yelled, "Mama, look, the train is gobbling up the tracks."

Rose turned around at hearing the child's voice -- and yes, the front of the engine did look like a heavy growth of whiskers.

After a long period of separation, Uncle John just couldn't quit talking. We got in the carriage to drive to the hotel. It was called 'Hotel Albert.' "I never dreamed a building like this would exist at the end of the world! Carnelia, remember the time we went to Venice? It looks exactly like the Doge's Palace."

"Well, it's supposed to," said her great uncle. "It was built about thirteen years ago, back in '59; 'should'a seen it during the last war we had with the Yanks. It was turned into a hospital for Confederate officers and soldiers, with nurses running round all over the place. But in April '65, the Yankee raiders came lashing through the town, burning and destroying all in their path -- was the same day Richmond, Virginia, evacuat-

Albert Hotel was copied from Doge's Palace at Venice

ed, as did Selma, and the Confederacy. Then General Wilson and his bunch took over the hotel rooms to map out their plans for a march through Montgomery where they would ride on to meet General Sherman in Georgia. Enough of that though. What I want to see you about is the Edleigh Estate. You meet with me and my lawyer tomorrow. I have no other kin, so I'm making you my legal heir. There are some stocks and bonds and small pieces of real estate, my lands in England are still let out to tenants. I'm getting quite feeble, as you can see... and I'd like to be assured that you and your daughter get your inheritance."

"Uncle John, you don't have to do all that: we are comfortably situated. Aren't there some charities here that you'd like to give to?"

"I've got no friends here, boy. Somehow they never took to outsiders. Have been here now for thirty years and guess I don't know anyone but the maid and my driver -- and I think my barber's name is MacDonald... or one of those dern Scottish names."

"I'll bet you haven't tried to like your neighbors, have you?" chimed in Rose, "It's a two-way thing, y'know."

"When you've rested up, we'll go out and see the Poderfoy property. It's out by the big cemetery where some mighty powerful gentlemen are buried. Sometimes I think that's why the house stays vacant so much. They say ghosts prowl around the area at night."

"Uncle, did you know our Rose is a concert pianist? She teaches at the Royal Academy of Music and has played several times at the Queen's request. I wouldn't be surprised if we were not in America again soon on concert tour."

"Well, she comes by it naturally, her great grandmother was good on the Harpsichord. That old thing is still somewhere in London -- the instrument, I mean. I live at the Hotel Albert... we'll be on the same floor."

Rose and Carnelia were impressed with the hotel's interior: the high ceilings, the beautifully carved stairway, crystal chandeliers, the panelled walls, marble fireplace and the plush carpets. "Not bad," murmured Carnelia.

After sight-seeing the next day:... the mausoleum of the founder of the town; the Arsenal of the South; the place where the Marquis de Lafayette landed below the bluffs of the Alabama River in 1825; and on and on... "this is no 'hick-town'," said Rose.

"It's a beautiful town, Uncle John, but where did it get its name? I've never heard it before."

"When William Rufus King started the place in 1821 -- he had heard someone read the "Songs of Selma" by a Gaelic poet. Selma was an Indian Princess, and it was also the name of a thing that meant 'throne', and because the very high bluffs on the river made Mr. King think of a throne, he thought the poem suited the City."

"That's so lovely. The bluffs make me think of the 'Pallisades' we saw in New York and also the 'Cliffs of Dover' in England."

Tomorrow was the day of their departure if they were to be back in London by September. The return trip seemed shorter -- and sorta' sad, too.

"I behold thy towers, O Selma!
The oaks of thy shaded wall:
Thy streams sound in my ear;
Thy heroes gather round."
    ---McPherson's "Poems of Ossian"

William Rufus King cir. 1820

CHAPTER 11

The Academy

Rose had just enough time to pack and get back to the faculty's dormitory before registration of new students. After settling in, she sent a message to Arthur Sullivan saying she wanted to resume her study with him. She found some of the new students unqualified for the level that the Academy required. In these situations she felt discomfort in confronting the candidate. But one girl appealed to her in such earnestness that she finally told her she would teach her privately on her own until she caught up on the skills demanded by the school. Rose would never regret this decision; in nine months the student was like a different person. A deep affection developed between them, and when she went to Hampstead for an occasional weekend she would take Katherine with her. The game of tennis had been played in Italy, France, and England in the 16th century and was still popular in England. Katherine would make a good fourth for doubles. Barnabus was soon educated to the fact that the balls were not served for him to 'go fetch' when one day Father whammed a well-aimed ball right at Barn's rear! He went off the court, with his tail tucked, to the stables to commiserate with Champion, the oldest of the mares.

Sullivan told Rose at her next session, about his idea of making *Ivanhoe*, by Walter Scott, into a grand opera. He would do it independently of Gilbert. They didn't always see eye to eye -- so she was to say nothing to anyone about his project.

Mr. Edleigh was in London and met Rose for lunch. He ordered for both, then took from his case a letter postmarked Nürnberg, Germany.

"Oh, Father, let me see it. It would be from the Rhinhardts, Fritz's parents." She ripped open the envelope and deciphered the German contents:

Dear Rose:

Papa and I received your kind letter. Thank you for writing. The bad memories are fading -- and are leaving a sweet fragrance of our dear son's life. We wish that we had not been selfish in wanting Fritz to settle here close to us, but we loved him so! When we go to church we pray for you -- that your life can be happy.

A news bulletin announced a musical program that would be held in Nürnberg, financed by the faculty of the Royal Academy of Music where you teach. Will you be performing? If so, come and stay with Papa and me. It would mean so much to talk with someone who shared in our loving remembrance of Fritz.

Maria Rhinhardt

Rose carefully placed the letter in its envelope and put it in her bag. "Father, I'm not very hungry."

"But it's very light fare -- and you must eat something. Music demands a lot of stamina. Would you rather go to the Nürnberg Festival without us along?"

"Yes," and she picked up her fork and took a bite

or two.

"What are you playing in Germany -- something from your old repertory, or have you a new piece?"

"It's new, Father. Arthur thinks it's the best thing I've written yet; I'll play it for you when I come out to Hampstead. I can't believe it will soon be 1874!"

"Well, guess what! George du Maurier and Emma have a new son; they've named him Gerald. He's a pram-full, all right -- and a voice to match his size. We see quite a bit of them. When is your trip to Nürnberg?"

"I believe it is in April. Once a year the towns-people have a song fest in celebration of the old 16th century contests. They put their whole selves into the occasion, and are very demanding of the musician's skill. So I won't have much free time for weekends at home -- as I must polish and polish my number," she said.

"I didn't tell you that Barnabus has a new friend: a black and white cat that he dragged in one day and plunked at our feet. We've advertised for it's owner, but have come up with nothing. He really loves that thing. The two go walking in the park -- attracting a lot of attention. Well, I must be off, Love. Don't over-work!"

CHAPTER 12

Christmas arrived. Katherine joined them at Hampstead, as it was so far to Truro, her home. New Year's came. The du Mauriers spent January 1st with the Edleighs and he sang their favorite *Der Lieben Langer Tag* again for them.

April was almost on them. Rose hated packing and that sort of preparation for trips, but she knew it would be a bit cold, so she threw into her bag an extra sweater or two. They were off. The train took them to Dover and from there a ferry would land them in Ostende, Belgium. Then it would be a long, long trip by train. The Crown was sponsoring her, so there wasn't anything to worry about -- just go and enjoy. Each country sent its best representatives in music ability to the contests. The itinerary had been issued them: after they docked in Ostende, they would go by train to Brussels; fifty miles farther they would be in Liege, twenty more to Verviers; and seventy miles east to Bonn. The tour group stayed at a hotel and had a chance to see where Beethoven was born in 1770. Bonn was the gateway to the ethereal, romantic Rhine Valley, once called Castra Bonnensia, about two thousand years ago. In 253 A.D., Cassius and Florentius were martyred for their Christian beliefs. Where the Cathedral stands, one of the first shrines had been raised over their graves. Poppelsdorfer Castle is the home of Bonn's famous University. After dinner Rose and a group walked the promenade that extended along the Rhine banks from the Alter Zell to the German Parliament building, the Bundeshaus.

Off to the railway station the next morning for Koblenz, about forty miles away. The scenery was breathtaking, as rivers and mountains both converged here, and right where Koblenz stood is where the Mosel River ran into the Rhine. Rose had never been in these parts of Germany during her two year's study in Berlin. When you are learning music, you don't take trips like this. There were three mountain ridges: the Eifel to the north, Hunstrück to the south, and Westerwald to the east. She promised herself to return someday and sail southward on the Rhine. She, Carnelia and Father would visit the picturesque village and the forlorn romantic castles that dotted the shoreline. But now on to Mainz, sixty miles southeast. She believed the trains on the Continent were faster than their British ones. Arthur Sullivan sat next to Rose -- he produced a 'dumb keyboard' and advised her to use it to keep her fingers nimble. "But there's so much beauty in the scenery, I want to look."

"Why, you can do your scales and arpeggios in your sleep -- just keep those fingers moving. There's a world of competition that you've never dreamed of that will be in Nürnberg."

In Mainz, there were wonderful architectural structures in rococo style of the 18th century. Everything was in a florid design, curved lines and ornamentation in pierced shellwork that she could view from the coach window. She wondered if Fritz's friend William Tilly ever saw any of this. They were both studying architecture before the war, thought Rose.

"There's a university here named 'Gutenberg' after the early printer, inventor of moveable type in the late thirteen hundreds. Perhaps Mainz will be represented at the Nürnberg contest," said Sullivan. They were only going to switch tracks -- no time to look at anything. We'd be in Darmstadt for a late lunch.

"Now here I know we will have stiff competition, because this old cultured town is known worldwide for its musicians, especially for Friedrich von Flotow, best known for his opera, *Martha.* The school in London put it on the year before you entered. He is still living here and I bet we'll see him at the 'Song-fest'."

They were in the Neckar Valley now and the train was slowing for the village Eberbach; they could see the Neckar bridge from the window. Then the train picked up speed, flying toward Würzburg, a hundred miles away. Rose had some information about Würzburg. The brochure mentioned the area of Würzburg as having been inhabited over 120,000 years ago -- such statements always got the 'hum-bug' from Rose who was a staunch fundamentalist when it came to dates farther back than Genesis. She didn't believe the archaeologist-theory on the age of Stonehenge in England. She'd accept the Celts living in their hearth-heated huts who built a fortress on the top of their hill where the present old castle stands, and the Germanic tribes settling on the site of the city at the start of the Christian Era. Kilian of Ireland became their first missionary -- called the Apostle of the Franks. The Frankish duchess rejected Christianity and had him and his two brothers put to death. In spite of this, in 742, Würzburg became a bishopric -- a little later acquiring secular power as well. The Prince-bishops ruled the city for a thousand years. Walter von der Vogeltery, the famous Minnesinger died at the monastery in 1230. Rose was eager to go in the Residenz to see the carvings; the Grand stairway with the ceiling painted by Tiepolo; and the Hofkirche.

Tomorrow their group would arrive in Nürnberg, with a day to rest before the Music-fest. The townspeople had turned over their spare rooms to the visiting musicians. But Rose got a hack to drive her to the Rhinhardts. When they heard the carriage drive up they ran to the street to greet her. Rose was dumbfounded, for there was William Tilly also. He had come for the event when the Rhinhardts had told him Rose would play at the contest. There were outbreaks of laughter intermingled with tears. Maria Rhinhardt thought Rose would be very tired, so after a light supper, there was an early retirement. Bright the next morning, a breakfast tray was brought to her bed, but she was already up and dressed and asked if she might join the rest in the dining room. William did most of the talking, as he had to translate lots of the conversation. Today's events were for the vocal artists and tomorrow's would be the pianists and other instrumentalists. The third day, the awards would be given out.

Rose went to the Rhinhardt's piano and practiced for two hours. When she finished, she felt satisfied about her playing.

The entire town had gone overboard for the festival. Banners and streamers waved from every upright or over-head column. Where did so many people come from! But there was order and friendliness -- everybody excited, but all under control. The Rhinhardts, William Tilly and Rose walked over to the square. The contestant's names were listed on sheets of paper that were passed out. In twenty minutes the program started. A hush fell over the assemblage; and the soprano from Vienna began her aria from *La Traviata* -- a great favorite among the music lovers. Her ovation was good. The next singer was from a small town in France; she sang "The Lass With the Delicate Air" by Thomas Arne. Rose whispered to William, "Arne is from my country."

At the long judge's stand, there was much note-taking and suspense. The third entry was a girl from Würzburg, Germany, with too much assurance about herself. When she started on "The Wren", a buzzing insect started on an obligato accompaniment. She slapped at the pest several times, losing her poise, then all of a sudden she was choking and blushing. Her accompanist went to her side and led her off stage. No one booed or derided her.

There was a break in the schedule for recess, so all dispersed for a lunch they had brought with them. The contest would be resumed in an hour. The Würzburg diva was being given another chance, and this time, having won the admiration of the crowd in showing such pluck, was applauded with great enthusiasm.

Seven contestants comprised today's list, all the people left the square in mid-afternoon. There was much discussion among the town's group and visitors as to the merits of each participant.

Rose was not yet labeled a 'professional artist' so she was still able to qualify in the trials. But this would be her last chance, probably. When they reached their host's home Rose and William had a private conversation. The Franco-Prussian War was tough, but didn't last long. He was able to return to Berlin and finish his degree and was now placed with a well-known Architectural firm -- in fact there were rumors that he might come along on the job in England at St. Albans, north of London. Rose's eyes lit up, "Oh, William, that will be marvelous, that's only a short distance from Hampstead and you could visit us on the weekends. We have horses, a dog, Barnabus, and he has a friend -- a cat -- that goes everywhere with him. In fact, when he got caught in the fork of the tree branches Barn almost broke the tree down to free him before Father could get to them. I have a young student at the Academy who goes home with me occasionally, but space is no problem with us. Please work on your superior to allow you to come on the project!"

"I couldn't think of anything nicer, Rose. But here come our host and hostess, let's change the subject to the Music-fest."

Tomorrow's program would last all day, as so many instrumentalist were signed up. "Play for us what you will be doing," said Mr. Rhinhardt.

"Yes, I'll be happy to. I call it 'Farewell to Spring'," and she sat at the piano for a moment thinking it wasn't a good selection for grieving parents... but she began to play. When the last note faded away, the three of them embraced her; there was a lump in Mr. Rhinhardt's throat when he vowed that she had that

trophy in her hands! "I know how the audience reacts...
I've been to every one for the last forty years."

They would have supper in, and afterwards talk
and cry a little and laugh a little. Then to bed for the
next day's contest. As the host said goodnight, he declared, "As for you two young people, Art is a high and
holy avocation -- remain true to it. Sleep well."

The day dawned with streams of lovely sunshine
falling across Rose's bed. She got to her knees and
thanked the Creator for all the beauty in life... "and
even at the threshold of death may we glimpse a bit of
the glory of the presence of Jesus Christ through Whom
all things are possible, Amen."

She arose, dressed carefully in the simple, but
becoming dress and went downstairs to greet the others.
"Last night I had the funniest dream: our big Barnabus
(a St. Barnard) went out and caught a rat and brought
it to his feline friend... he just pushed it away. It hurt
Barn's feelings, so he ran off. I wonder if there's any
significance to it!"

"Oh, dreams generally mean just the opposite of
what you see in them... I'll bet it was the other way
around; kitty caught the mouse and your Barnabus
turned up his nose at it."

Rose ate with a good appetite. In two hours she
would be at the piano before thousands of people.

The moment finally came. She was calm -- after
all, music was for folk's happiness. So she started on
her 'original composition' -- and much attention was
drawn to that fact. Every ear strained -- and her fingers gave wing to her heart. Her tones were clear, and
the cadenzas brilliant. She felt her audience singing
along with her and she loved playing for them! When
she finished, such a roar of praise arose -- none had

heard the likes of since the old Minnesinger's days.

The judges looked at each other in accord; but it wasn't over yet. There were six more to be heard. It didn't seem quite fair to have to follow the object of such an adoring audience that Rose had captured. But he took his turn and did his best on the clarinet. The response was polite -- five more to go. After the last number, the next contestant had a better advantage. She was a violinist from Romania, and how those Slavs can make your heart bleed!

"This is going to be stiff for our Rose," whispered William to his host.... "We'll see," is all Mr. Rhinhardt would say.

The next four seemed to run through their selections with jaded enthusiasm. The judges thanked them all and placed wreaths of flowers around the shoulders of all participants and announced, "Tomorrow at one o'clock." The crowd seemed larger than ever -- some now yielding to a mug of beer: it was a day of festivity.

Next day the Chief judge faced the crowd -- waving those assembled to hush them. "Please, please, we've had difficulty in making a decision -- we can only break the tie between a pianist and a violinist by having them play again." Never was such tension felt in so great a mass of humanity. "Miss Edleigh of London, England, and Miss Katrina Melnikoff of Romania, will you come forward. We will have an encore from each and make our selection."

Before advancing to the stage both girls put their heads together, and since music is such an international language they had no difficulty conveying their thoughts. Rose looked at Katrina with mischief in her eyes and Katrina giggled back at her. They both strode out arm in arm and the violinist and pianist started improvising on a piece that everyone in the civilized world knew from childhood. Rose whispered, "key of A Major" and played several bars of the "Barcarolle" from *Tales of Hoffman* and Katrina joined in. There came such a response from the people -- some with tears flowing down their cheeks -- some humming -- some whistling the melody. The heavens rang with all the joyful noise, everybody loved the two performers. At the conclusion of the piece... "bravo, encore, more!" could have been heard in the next village. The tied first-placers bowed, then struck out with Martin Luther's "A Mighty Fortress is Our God," with thousands of voices joining in. Nürnberg had never experienced such a Music-fest! The judges were spell-bound. What to do! The first judge came out to announce that a decision had been made. The prize would be split.

The Rhinhardts, Arthur Sullivan and William tore their way through the body of excited humanity and helped Rose off the stage. Katrina and her parents joined them for a supper in the village restaurant. "This is a day Nürnberg will never forget," toasted Mr. Rhinhardt.

Life seems to be made up of hellos and good-byes. But it was time to retrace those long train tracks. She was taking honor back to the Academy and that would repay the Queen for sponsoring her and her teacher. After settling in the coach, and drawing a deep breath Rose turned to her companion. "Thank you, Arthur, you made it all possible for me."

"No, dear... and I've been awaiting the right moment to tell you this: Franz Liszt has written me, asking about your composition progress. By now he has heard about your work from the news releases from Nürnberg. That was the most unselfish act that I've

ever noticed among egotistical young artists... the way
you and Katrina settled the tie. You taught people the
true meaning of music. Your names will be talked of
all over Europe. Now, what I want to speak to you
about: I think a year under Liszt will be the best thing
for you -- the notoriety is important to the concert
background. Can you be spared the time off at the
Academy? And will your finances allow the expenses
involved?"

"Yes, my father has come into an inheritance... I
don't know the worth, but Carnelia will also help out
until I'm on my feet. I think money is no problem."

"Then we better make preparations for next year.
The public still likes them young and winsome. Liszt is
now living forty-five miles northeast of Nürnberg, in
Bayreuth, where his close friend, Wagner, has established a great Opera House."

CHAPTER 13

London

Many, many hours later they pulled into Waterloo Station, both very tired. Rose was met by her father and Carnelia. They dropped Arthur Sullivan at his residence on the way to their flat... "We'll not talk too much tonight, but go straight to bed and at breakfast you can catch us up on everything. We're so proud of you. The London papers carried the story on the Music-fest and one of the Queen's subjects winning the co-title of "best musician in Europe," said Father.

Rose slept so heavy and long that she had to be awakened for lunch the next day. At noon she unloaded everything on them -- how Liszt was interested in taking her as a student. "Do you think it could be worked out?"

"Of course. You must go to the top, if that's where your destiny lies, and Mr. Sullivan has advised us on the matter... no money costs should stop you," answered Carnelia.

Monday Rose was back in her faculty quarters, and after many congratulations things returned to normal. Class recitals were in session and her students did well, proving her ability as a good teacher. Now school was out for summer vacation, and Rose took off to Hampstead where she could stretch and breathe. Champion was getting too fat -- he needed riding more.

118

Barnabus followed behind on the trail. His Cat had left. "That's funny, I had a peculiar dream one night in Nürnberg, but it was just the opposite -- Barn left instead. Somebody said that dreams were most of the time that way. By the way, Father, Katherine is coming up next week, she isn't going home to Truro, but is going to take courses during the summer at the Academy."

"Oh, there is a letter from William Tilly. It's postmarked St. Albans," interrupted her father.

"I'll bet he is coming to visit us; we talked about the possibility of his Company doing a project in England. Maybe we will be having Katherine and William at the same time... my two dearest friends."

The second day after Katherine's arrival at Rose's home, a cable came saying that William would be there on Tuesday if convenient for them, if not he'd stay at an inn. Tuesday was the next day. After all the introductions they went into the garden for tea. Tomorrow they would go riding -- and in the afternoon a musical. The new housemaid delivered a note to the du Mauriers to join them. Life was rich and wonderful.

Katherine and William formed a warm friendship -- that Rose guessed would go deeper than 'just friends.' When William left Hampstead he asked Katherine if he might see her in London.

"You said 'yes' of course." Summer was gone in a flash. Rose was packing for Bayreuth to study with Liszt. It was to become the most wonderful time of her life. Her days were full; her teacher was demanding, but so kind. He presented her in four concerts -- two with orchestras... a work she already knew, and the other two he had arranged when Wagner visited him in Bayreuth. Liszt told Rose all about Wagner's 'angel',

Ludwig II, who at the last moment of Wagner's monetary crisis in building Bayreuth's Festspielhaus (opera house) came up with necessary funds. "Perhaps you will meet King Ludwig when he comes to attend the presentation of Wagner's *Ring*. This cycle includes the operas *Die Walküre*, and *Siegfried*, *Du Götterdammering*, and *Das Rheingold*, four dramas written about legends from an old German poem known as *Nibelungen Lied*." It would open this August. That would be 1876, Rose would soon be thirty-two. "Maestro, does it always take one so long to reach her goal in music?"

"My Dear, some are born geniuses, and, for greedy vanity on the parent's part, are exploited at a very early age. Their brilliance soon fades like a shooting star that falls somewhere into oblivion. You are fortunate not to have been reared in that atmosphere. What you have is solid and lasting... let's keep it like that, just growing and becoming stronger. When we older ones are gone, you will be here to carry on, Rose." (She could not dream of how soon that day was to come: Wagner would lie in rest in his beautiful garden at his home in Bayreuth in 1883, and Franz Liszt would be dead in 1886.) Liszt spoke of his own great teacher, "When I was nine years old, my father recognized my talent and placed me with the most famous teacher in Vienna, Salieri."

"If my lesson period is up, I want to ask you a question about Ludwig II. Why was he called a King when Bavaria is part of Germany?"

"Good question. King Ludwig was admired by Bismarck and appreciated for his cultivating the Arts. So Bismarck allowed Bavaria its independence as long as everything went along smoothly with Bismarck's and the Prussian King's plans. So you see how important the Arts are."

"Yes, thank you, sir."

Time flowed through the hourglass like mercury on a greased tilted surface. Months had been spent in Bayreuth, seeming as only days. And spring was here with three of the four concerts behind her; and fame was on its way. Every few days, there would be letters from home, which she read and reread. Barnabus had placed his footprint on one of them... which made her smile and get that old nostalgia for the beloved simplicity of home. "And oh, Barn's Cat is back," added the postscript.

Rose practiced three to four hours a day, took a long walk, and spent the remaining time with reading or writing letters. Father and Carnelia would arrive the third of August to attend the Grand Opening of Wagner's Festspielhaus -- and that was not far away.

All of Bayreuth was preparing for the event. Word had leaked out that the King of Bavaria would be present; flags and flowers were everywhere, but Ludwig, who hated crowds, dinner parties and adoring audiences, foiled them all by taking an early train, and by previous arrangement arrived at one a.m. at an inn a mile away from Bayreuth. Wagner, who was waiting, greeted his dear friend whom he'd not seen in eight years. The King and composer rode away in a royal carriage to the Hermitage, the palace of the Margraves. Ludwig would be staying there during the festival.

After the performance of the *Ring*, Ludwig wrote a letter to Wagner declaring his "thirst for the *Ring* was unquenched"... he must return to Bayreuth for the final cycle at the end of August... if he could be protected from the crushing crowds and assured that he could be there in privacy from the public eye.

Ludwig II of Bavaria

Wagner responded to his letter, but begged Ludwig to please show himself to the people who loved him so. They wanted to thank him for all he'd done for them. When he returned in late August, the King took Wagner's advice and stepped to the front to join in the applause as Wagner appeared before the curtain. The composer warmly acknowledged his greatfulness to his patron. It did something for the eccentric, shy King -- perhaps that was the happiest he would ever be again. But this is not the story of the 'Dream King' of Bavaria.

Carnelia was wild to see Munich and the Bavarian country. So with the consent of Liszt, Rose would take off two weeks to tour the sights of southern Germany. They passed through Nürnberg and would approach Munich from the north. The weather was perfect and first off they would find a moderate hotel with old atmosphere. They wanted to feel the soul of the city, visit the beer gardens and listen to the tongue-twisting sounds of Germans in their relaxed moods. Rose wanted to see the baroque castle of Nymphenburg, the summer residence of the Kings of Bavaria. It was here in 1845 that Maria, a princess of Prussia, had given birth to the boy who would become Ludwig II. Not far away nestled between hills and lakes was a romantic castle called Hohenschwangau where the Royal family went in the spring months. It had been bought in 1832 in a terrible condition and renovated by the best builders in the Budermeier style -- a partly Gothic interpretation. Swans were the motif, the young boy's room was decorated with German legends. All the walls were murals of Knights of the Holy Grail... on which Wagner later based his opera, *Lohengrin.* So the Edleighs decided that would be their first day's excursion.

Never had they seen anything so breath-taking. That night they stayed in Füssen, close to the castle. Tomorrow it would be to Lake Starnberg; Rose wanted to visit Possenhofen, the home of Elizabeth, Empress of Austria, King Ludwig's first cousin. Elizabeth and Ludwig were very close friends before she married Emperor Franz Josef -- and had ridden horseback together around the banks of the lake. There they saw her home; next door was a smaller place whose owner was Oskar von Miller, an engineer John Edleigh knew only through communications with his office at the Exchange in London. He would like to meet him if he was at home. They stopped the cabby and John went up to the front door and knocked. Von Miller's son answered and John introduced himself.

"My father is expected very shortly, will you step inside and wait?"

"Well, I have my wife and daughter with me, I will consult with them. I must ask where you learned your fluent English from."

"We had classes at the school I attended, and then I studied in your country last year."

The Edleighs had told their driver to take his leisure for an hour or so at the tavern and return for them. In a few minutes Oskar von Miller came through the entrance and greeted his guests. "John Edleigh, why of course, from the Royal Exchange! What a real pleasure to meet you. I have many things to talk with you about; you must all stay for dinner."

The kitchen was alerted for three more places at the table. "Perhaps Rudolph could take Rose for a sail on the lake, if she wishes."

"She wishes very much, Sir, I'd like to sail in front of Berg Castle where King Ludwig spends some of his time -- then back by the front of Possenhoffen."

"That can be done, and be back in time for dinner," said Rudolph.

She couldn't know that she would have reason for remembering this excursion in just a few years hence.

"You will certainly spend the night with us," said the hostess. "We can send the stable boy to the tavern to bring your driver here... as you see we have much room." This had to be translated, as Mrs. Miller knew little of English. It was easier to say yes than to argue -- so all slept wonderfully with the lake to view upon awakening the next morning. John Edleigh listened to his host speaking of his dreams to build the greatest museum in the world on natural science and technology in Munich. "I want the visitor to be able to follow production methods from their start to the finish by fascinating models and displays for scientific research."

Most men would have given up their dreams before von Miller's became a reality. In the first place, money was hard to raise -- and the King of Bavaria was more interested in romantic, fantastic follies and would sponsor nothing in the world of reality.

That morning, the Edleighs felt it necessary to make an early departure. After all, they had acted a bit brash by barging in on them, but the eighteen year old son and Rose seemed to have enjoyed it tremendously. Rose's nature was to find pleasure in people of all ages.

"Again, please -- and soon," insisted von Miller.

"Yes, and England is yours!" And they rode away to Munich. The rest of the day they viewed the exquisiteness of the landscaping. On the left bank of the Isar River was the bronze statue of Maximilian II, father of Ludwig II and his nuttier brother Otto. Crossing the Maximilian Bridge and to the right was the new Maximilianeum, being built for the King. Their driver told them in broken English -- and much sign language -- that during the 'Thirty Year's War' the Swedes had taken over Munich, but did not destroy it, as was their usual custom. In 1638, out of gratitude, the Elector of Bavaria erected the Mariensäule, a column in marble adorned with the statue of the Madonna. Rose wanted to go to the little church of St. John Nepomuk that was built by the Asam brothers out of funds from their own pockets. The great ceiling painting inside was astounding -- and the rococo style was as beautiful as she remembered Fritz telling about; he'd gone there several times to study some architectural feature. Rose had been thinking about Fritz a lot on this trip. It was that way when she stayed away from the piano for very long.

The next day she would start back to Bayreuth. The train took them to Nürnberg, a hundred miles... then by coach to Bayreuth, about sixty more. Wearily they finally reached Rose's quarters, saturated with enough culture for the time being. John and Carnelia would leave the following day for England. Carnelia said, "Don't you wish we could just board an eagle's back and fly home!" "Yep, that's some highfalutin idea you're dreaming up," said her mate.

Rose went to her lesson the day the Edleighs left. Liszt had a proposition to offer: would she take over the corrections on his compositions and proofing of them before they went to press. Her study with him would be in exchange for these services. He would also obtain concerts for her, so she could be financially independent. He was a father-image to her -- his kindness and regard helped in the absence of family. Here she was... thirty-five years old and needing filial dependence. The thing was, she was a child at heart. Rose became a close friend to Cosima, Liszt's daughter who was married to Richard Wagner. In 1880 a pianist canceled out on a performance at the Music Hall and Liszt immediately substituted Rose. Her performance was magnificent and won the praise of the visiting Prince of Esterhazy, whose family had been responsible for giving Liszt his start when he was only nine years old. (Liszt's father was given a thousand dollars a year for his study under Randhartinger and Salieri.) After attracting the attention of the Esterhazy nobility, concert offers came frequently to Rose.

In August, a bulky letter arrived from England. It was from Carnelia.

My darling Rose,

We read about your splendid ascendancy into Royalty. The Esterhazys seem to have taken you under their wings. Don't lose our sweet Rose with all that adulation and praise! You don't realize how much your father misses his sweet girl. He visualizes you at the end of your program coming on stage and spreading your skirt for a curtsy... like when you were nine.

I hate to write this, but you will have to know sooner or later. Champion had to be put down. The new stableman's son was out exercising him and the poor beast tripped over a branch and was thrown to the ground, breaking his leg. Old 'Doc' was called and upon examining him said there was nothing that could be done. He was suffering terribly and we decided it was cruel to let him go on like that. 'Doc' shot him and we buried him right where he fell. Barnabus spends most of his time snuggled up with his head on his grave. Cat returned to us and frequently keeps vigil with him. There always has to be a smile though, even when it seems everything goes wrong: Cat caught a mouse and took it to old Barn to comfort him. But I'm afraid he just hasn't good manners -- he scorned his offering. So we gave Cat a large ham bone to carry out to his friend -- and him a little one... they gnawed in good companionship.

And, oh, these things would never reach the papers there. Last year, the Queen's life was threatened by a criminal named Edward Madden. They tried him and found him of unsound mind; he had developed a mania for frightening sovereigns. It was discovered that he had threatened the lives of King Leopold, Emperor Franz Josef, President Johnson and Napoleon III. On May 12, the Queen's first great grandchild, daughter of the Princess of Saxe-Meininger, was born.

The Queen opened Parliament in person in February and left the next month for Baden-Baden and Darmstadt. Your favorite novelist, George Eliot, died in December. So many seem to be passing away -- soon there will be a void felt in the land.

When will you take a holiday to visit your home? Hampstead is sad without you. Remember, this is where you live!

(P.S.   I am enclosing several other
items you might like to read.)
                              Lovingly,
                              Carnelia

     Rose was sick at heart... she went to the keyboard
to dissolve her mood. She found her fingers wandering
over the keys in a most sad and sorrowful tune -- and
as her fingers moved she became more and more emo-
tional. She knew not where the melody came from...
something she'd heard or some experience of the past
expressing itself in music. But in the next moment
there was a knock on her door. It was a telegram from
London from Katherine Halcom saying that she and
William Tilly were going to be married. "The ceremony will be at St. Albans Abbey at Christmas time."
     Rose sat down and wrote Katherine immediately.
She was so excited -- her pen wouldn't move fast
enough, not stopping to correct but just scratching out
errors. "I want to know all about it... write me every
detail. Will you stop your music, will William's project
be finished, where will you live?
     "I'm doing very well in Bayreuth, have given sev-
eral concerts -- which, I dare say, helps one financially,
so that I don't have to call on Father. I will come
home in mid-December and we'll have a big party before the wedding. There's so much to talk about -- but,
of course, you have only one thing on your mind! Give
William my love. Affectionately, Rose."
     Liszt never ceased praising Rose on her ability --
it seemed she matured more each lesson: ...her phrasing, technique and professionalism. "Would you like to
play at the palace for the Emperor of Germany?" he
asked.

"If you think I'm right for it, I shall be happy to --
but when?"

"It will be in October for the October-fest," said
he.

"Yes, I wanted to know first, because I will take a
trip home for the December Holidays. My protégée
will be married to a dear old friend of mine."

"You astound me, Rose, my dear, you put everybody's pleasure before your own aggrandizement. That
is good, though. Art will await the spirit!"

When the Edleighs learned all the news
happening in Bayreuth and at St. Albans they joined in
on the excitement. Writing to Rose, Carnelia told her
she'd get her an evening gown that would knock the
Emperor's eyes out! And as for the wedding -- she
expected its activity to take place at their home in
Hampstead, as Katherine's mother was not living.

Much correspondence passed back and forth from
London, to Bayreuth, to Hampstead in the month of
September. The weather was still warm in the day, but
the evenings cooled off. Rose worked hard so as not to
shame her teacher before the King.

Liszt suggested she do the "Rhapsody in E Flat"
by Brahms and one of her own compositions -- perhaps
the "Sad Song", and to have an encore number in mind.

By the middle of September the package arrived
containing the dress Carnelia had selected for her performance. It was an ice-blue shimmering satin with off-
shoulder line and a full sweep to the skirt. The trim
was a deeper blue border of velvet rosebuds edging the
neckline and skirt; the bodice was very tiny and maintained with stays beneath. There was a short plumage
of ostrich feather fastened to a cluster of roses for her
upswept hair-do. She put it on and stood before the

mirror... "Well, Rose, I didn't know you were pretty! If the Emperor doesn't like my playing, he has to like the costume!"

Liszt picked her up an hour before they were due and rode around a while to relax her in the fresh air. When the festival guests had assembled in the hall, all the lights were glittering... Rose would never forget the experience. She faced the Royal box and bowed low. She moved toward the piano, and brushing everything from her mind and concentrating on the Brahms piece -- she released all her energy on the keyboard. She felt confident that she was performing her best. Upon finishing, the Emperor stood in gratitude of her personal sacrifice for her talent. Liszt was not a young man any more so he didn't stay for the reception afterwards; he told Rose to linger on a while with Cosima and Richard Wagner... they would see her home. It was the most charming evening of her life and one long to be cherished.

A gentleman stepped up to her and presented her with an important-looking container... he looked at her then nodded in the direction of the donor. On opening it the sparkles leaped out, almost blinding her with the precious stones of the necklace. It was a gift from the Emperor.

Later she showed it to Franz Liszt, who commented that their brilliance was dull compared to her gift to the Emperor of her music. The chill in the air meant that it was almost time for her trip home. It was difficult to concentrate on anything but the glorious holidays to come soon. She couldn't believe that she was not far from forty years old -- and so contented. The memories of Fritz were still there, but they were sweet... like a lovely dream... and would comfort her all her life. No one thought of her as an "old maid" or an "available lady". One moment she was like a madonna and the next a little child.

And it was the little child that was traveling over the tracks from Bayreuth to Ostende, across the channel, and on to Hampstead Heath. Here she would be in another world... a universe that was peopled with Father, Carnelia, Barnabus, Cat, Begonia... she would visit the graves of Champion and beloved Nanny of her childhood.

The house was already festive for the Christmas holidays with wreaths of holly, mistletoe on chandeliers, ivy around the staircase and sweet-smelling candles everywhere. Rose flopped to the floor and rolled over with Barnabus, scratching his ears -- and he licking her cheeks. What a sight... only months ago she was accepting a priceless gift from the Emperor!

There were letters for her on the foyer table. She ripped open the one from Katherine first and read:

My dear Friend,

I will reach Hampstead on the 19th of
December. How wonderful of you to do all
this for me -- but I'm just in a dream world.

Your own,
Katherine

Carnelia and Rose put their heads together over the wedding plans. "We can have the wedding party here. I am so glad they changed their plans about St. Albans Abbey Church, as the transportation would have been a problem. The Reverend Aston could marry them in the little Parish Church, or if that's too small, we can use St. John's Wood Church on Wellington Road. I don't know if William's relatives could come so far in the cold weather, but he will have friends at the place of his employment. We'll count on about six of them. The du Mauriers can put up several at their home... unless they would rather stay at the Spaniards Inn. Gerald is the name of the du Maurier's little son -- well, I guess he is almost eleven now. He comes over to ride the horses occasionally -- he's a very good-looking, well behaved young fellow. Old Barn just adores him -- Cat has no use for anybody much, but his own household. Well, if we reach more than fifty in number of guests we'll have to hire a hall close to here."

Excitement continued -- finally the eighteenth of December came. William Tilly arrived early so that he could go into London to get Katherine at the Academy.

When there was a lull in all the activity Carnelia told Rose that in the past September President Garfield of the U.S.A. had been the victim of an assassin; he died after a long and painful struggle. There was great sympathy shown in England. The Queen's Court went into mourning, a custom rarely observed for any but the Crowned heads. President Garfield's bier was adorned with the largest and most beautiful wreath ever seen; it bore a card: "Queen Victoria to the memory of the late President; sympathy for Mrs. Garfield and the American Nation."

William and Katherine arrived at Hampstead on December 19. Everything was shining and twinkling for the holidays and Katherine felt like she was in fairyland. The next day the men, including William's friends and John Edleigh, George du Maurier plus a trailing Barnabus went horseback riding: it was warm for the season of the year. The ladies all enjoyed a tea party: Begonia rose to her culinary heights for the occasion with her scones, crumpets, and chocolate cakes.

The next day was Sunday and the largest carriage was used to accommodate the visitors. Time flew by and the wedding day was on them. Rose asked Katherine to wear the necklace that the Emperor of Germany had presented to her. Her dress was of delicate net, trimmed with festoons of white roses over a slip of rich gros de Naples, and she wore a garland of white roses crowning her long brown tresses. She insisted on a simple ceremony with Carnelia and Rose playing the wedding music. The moment arrived. While the guests assembled, Carnelia played Bach's "Arioso" and Schubert's "Ave Maria." Then the minister asked the congregation to kneel and pray silently for the two who were to be united until death parted them -- and for the blessing of a happy home together, always adoring the Father in heaven Who brought them together and Who would hold them in sweet harmony. When the soft music stopped they all arose and turned to watch Katherine and William walk to the altar. The service of the marriage vows then proceeded with the Church liturgy. After they were pronounced 'man and wife', William lifted her veil and kissed her tenderly. They turned to the guests and bowed before walking back down the long aisle while the congregation sang "Love Divine, All Love Excelling" -- then into a rousing burst of "God Save the King."

The wedding party went to the Edleigh's for the reception. And judging from the empty champagne bottles all had a wonderful time! Farewells followed -- and by the time guests had departed, Katherine had changed into a traveling outfit. They told no one where they would be. Cornwall -- probably, as both shared so much interest in the past about that peculiar Duchy across the Tamar River. Though Katherine was born

Cat has no use for anybody but his own household
(From old engraving)

Old Barn just adores him

there she never got to travel and see its intriguing
beauty.

There was a quiet Christmas Eve at Rose's home.
Every member of the household seemed to be spending
a lot of time in his own room -- rattling papers and
dropping scissors... and all of a sudden prettily wrapped
packages appeared under the Christmas tree. Barnabus
took a few sniffs at the fresh green yew foliage; Cat did
a bit of investigating -- in fact, he disgraced himself by
batting at one of the precious antique baubles fastened
on the branch. In trying to reach it, he knocked off
three other ones that had belonged to John's mother.
They had been in the family since his grandfather's
time. Cat was going to spend the rest of Christmas in
the barn. He knew that for a fact, so he had already
scatted out of the house to his detention quarters.

The stockings were hung by the chimney with care
-- in hope no one put much there! They only wanted to
be together like old times. Perhaps George, Emma and
Gerald would stop in for refreshments and sing some
carols -- that would just make the evening complete.

CHAPTER 14

George du Maurier

Before New Year's came, Rose was tracking back to Bayreuth. She wondered if the newlyweds sent announcements to the Rhinhardts in Nürnberg and to Louisa, who used to play ensembles with Fritz, William and herself. She resumed her schedule and got down to some hard work. It was the year that the Queen of England, accompanied by Princess Beatrice, was entering her carriage at Windsor Station (after returning from London) that she was fired at by Roger Maclean. He was immediately arrested. Thank God she was not injured! He was from a respectable family... After trying him, they pronounced him not guilty of high treason by reason of insanity. He was confined for as long as the Queen had thought him out of danger to society.

Rose took over four of Liszt's students, as he was overworked -- and with her own practicing she found little time for memories. She had told Carnelia the day that Katherine had married that she felt it was Fritz and herself standing at the altar.

A little matter bothered Rose. She wanted to talk to her father, but never got the chance: what to do with the expensive necklace. She couldn't bear to own such an extravagant thing when some people were in need of a meal. She asked Liszt to put it in his safety vault for the present time. He thought that a wise decision, but that she should write her father as to what to do later. It was approaching spring -- her students were doing well. It was wonderful to be a good teacher. The term-recitals would soon be over and she would go home for the summer.

In England... that island of fleecy blue skies and dark heavy yew trees -- hillsides with their heaped-up stone boundaries looking from a distance like patch-worked quilts -- those streams glistening in the sunlight -- Mr. Edleigh knelt among his roses inspecting them for aphids. There was a click at the gate and George du Maurier walked down the bricked pathway. John looked up and grinned, "Come in, fellow, Holland is about to serve tea," as he pulled up two garden chairs. "Have been missing you lately; must have been out of town," said the host.

"Yes, I have been on a nostalgic journey back to the past when I was a boy and lived in Paris in an apartment in the rue de Passy. It was on a corner, and from the balcony I could look down on the rue de la Pompe. My father decided on this particular building because it had once been a blacksmith's laboratory where the owner worked at his hobby making locks and keys. There was a garden in back similar to the one where we are sitting that was a delight to me as a child. The gate in the wall led to a private avenue with tangled underbrush from which emitted the sweetest aroma of flowers. This was my land of mystery. Running parallel behind it was the Bois de Boulogne. Oh, the happy times my brother and I had! Someday soon I will put my notes together in a new book. You know, John, we were not titled people. The whole supposed-grandeur is a sham. My grandmother was English -- a Mary Anne Clark, born about 1776. She was the paramour of the Duke of York, and made certain that her son and daughter, resulting from this liaison, knew of their bloodline. Mary Anne was a blackmailer, receiving her livelihood from the Duke. Finally, she was paid-off and swore not to keep any of the Duke's letters. But they didn't know Mary Anne! She held back a few epistles for a 'rainy day'. Mary Anne left... or... rather, was exiled from... England for France with her son, George Noel and daughter Ellen. Ellen married Louis-Mathurin, a son of Mathurin-Robert Busson du Maurier. I was the son of this union. My father was consumed with the idea of a portable lamp -- which came to nothing. When we became émigrés, as a result of the National Convention decreeing that Louis Capet should suffer the death penalty, we departed for England. We assumed a title by adding the name "du Maurier" to Busson. The Bussons were only glass-blowers from earliest times. We adapted the suffix from a farm house of that name, understanding that 'le Maurier' meant a château. After many years I discovered that what was supposed to be a château was only a burnt-down large farm house. A difficulty arose when a member of a real château in that area -- the parish of la Fontaine St. Martin, near la Flèche belonging to the d'Orveaux family, came to London. My name was brought up somehow, and he, an officer who joined the Prince de Condé's army, appeared in London. I had a devil of a time for fear he would expose me. We, fortunately, moved in different circles so I was spared, as he was called back to France. It was important not to draw that attention when I was trying to make my way up with the news industry."

"Well, then we're both just commoners!" laughed John. "Here comes the tea. But where did you get your divine singing voice?"

"That was from my father. He sang when he worked, when he didn't work, when he dressed.... Maybe glass-blowing builds up a good set of lungs. And what do you hear from Rose?"

"She's to be home soon -- and I can't say how much joy she brings to our hearts when she's here. Be sure to bring over all the du Mauriers."

Cook would have a fit if she could see Mr. Edleigh feeding every other bite of shortbread to Barnabus, who would eat anything he could swallow... but Cat turned up his nose unless it swam or got around on four legs. He gave the gentlemen's ankles a rub and walked away.

"I must be going, the sun is dropping already."

A Summer in Cornwall

In June, Rose came home. It was a wonderful lazy summer. John, Carnelia, Rose and Begonia the cook, took off for Cornwall. They rented a cottage at Fowey where they planned to be for two months. Mapping out the itinerary was fun. The Great Western Railway would take them to Reading where they would spend the first night. Rose wanted to see the ruins of the great early 12th century Abbey, built by Henry I. She had studied in school about the earliest known piece of music ever written for several voices being composed by one of the monks here in 1240. The Abbey had been destroyed in the Great Rebellion. John wanted to stay at the George Hotel and get an early start the next day for Bristol, the famous old city situated on the Avon River. He wished to see a man he knew in the Royal Exchange who had moved here with the trade business, exporting goods to America and the West Indies. Rose and Carnelia went to see the old castle at the junction of the Avon and Frome Rivers. King Stephen had been a prisoner in 1141 for nine months. After early supper they took a look at St. Mary Redcliffe. Queen Elizabeth I had called this church "the fairest, the goodliest, and most famous parish church in England." There was much more to be seen than they had time for. Tomorrow they were scheduled to stay in Dorchester.

Rose was thrilled by the books of Thomas Hardy, who had started out as an architect, but turned to his real career of writing with his first novel, *Desperate Remedies* in 1871; *Under the Greenwood Tree*, 1872; *A Pair of Blue Eyes*, 1873; and *Far From the Madding Crowd*, 1874. "Father, perhaps we could meet him at Dorchester."

"I wouldn't count on it too much -- writers are most of the time eccentric," said John. Rose purchased everything by him that was in print. Hardy was born close to the town of Dorchester, at Melstock... not far from the Stinsford Church, where he made it the setting of his second novel. He was one of the singers in the Melstock choir, where he sang from the time he was a lad until he was a very old man.

Dorchester was the county seat of the shire of Dorset. "So this is the town of Judge Jeffreys who earned such a nasty reputation during the 'Bloody Assize' of 1685, when seventy-four of the Duke of Monmouth's adherents were sentenced to death and a hundred and seventy-five to transportation out of the country. If we could find a driver, we would go out to

Maiden Castle -- south of Dorchester. Near the railroad station is the largest of the pre-Roman amphitheaters in England and two miles from that is the renown pre-historic fortress of Maiden Castle -- not a real castle, but undulating circled hills that were used as a fortress by the Romans and Celts. Excavations have uncovered remains below ground of the Iron Age," added John.

The next day they took a hotel omnibus to the station and headed by train for Exeter -- 'that last outpost of civilization in the west', the townspeople boasted. "Maybe we'll stay here two days sight-seeing," said John. Early the next morning they started out for the Cathedral with it's great Norman towers. It dated from 1112 to 1206, with battlements and turrets added in the fifteenth century. The conventual church was first founded by Athelstan cir. 932 -- but was superseded by the rebuilt edifice; the only remaining feature of the original was the site and a few ground foundations. The chief object of interest was the tomb of Hugh Courtenay, Earl of Devon (died 1377) and his wife. As John knew the present Lord Courtenay, they would go to Powderham Castle on business transaction for the Exchange. First, a hansom cab was hired and they were driven to Castle Street to see the remains of Rougemont Castle erected by William the Conqueror. Carnelia was a Shakespearian enthusiast and asked them if they knew about Rougemont being referred to in the play *Richard III*. On the old Okehampton road, just outside Exeter, one would come to the park around Powderham Castle, built in 1390. After damage from the Civil War, it was restored in the 18th and 19th centuries by the Courtenays. Of course, they arrived at tea time (any time can be that in England).

The driver took them back to the Great Western Hotel. Their fifth day out from London would find them in Plymouth where they'd cross the Tamar River to Liskeard, Lostwithiel and to Fowey. Before reaching Plymouth they had passed through the town of Oke-hampton with its famous ruin of the Courtenay Earls; Lydford, an old Stannary town; Brentor, where there is a good view of the Brent Tor crowned with an ancient church -- then one enters the Tavy Valley. Tavistock was also a Stannary (center of a once important mining district). The Stannaries were selected by Edward I (1239-1307) for weighing and the stamping of tin. "The Prince of Wales," said John, "bore the title of Lord Warden of the Stannaries... and still does." Then on to Plymouth.

All were so tired by now that scenery meant little to them. "On the way back, we'll stop here and look around," continued John, as the others were yawning and nodding. The engine took on a different rhythm as it crossed the Royal Albert Bridge over the Tamar, then resumed its drowsy drone as it passed through the villages and farms, finally pulling in to Fowey. All the treasures would be explored later, but they only wanted to stretch out for about ten hours right now.

The sixth day they spent just lounging about the small inn while John Edleigh went to hire a hansom for the duration of their holiday. The cottage would be ready that night for them -- then they would be on their own. The little house contained three bedrooms and a large kitchen with eating nook. A screened porch would do for a sitting room. Three hammocks swung from the ceiling -- and there were two small boats tied up at the tiny pier in front of the cottage. "Oh, this is wonderful," exclaimed Rose, "I could live here forever!"

"Without your piano?" chimed in father. Begonia soon learned where to buy her groceries and enjoyed gossiping with the townspeople.

John told them that in the long ago times Fowey was one of the most favored seaports in the Kingdom. It had such a deep-water harbor that it would admit vessels of 13,000 tons. It shipped clay to all parts of the world for the making of pure white china. "You two city gals watch out when you start rowing away in those tiny boats -- got yourselves some life jackets?"

They loved lounging around, swinging in the hammocks, reading or talking, and Rose said, "You know, I wish Barnabus was here."

"I don't think that's a good idea with that coat of hair, unless you put a life preserver on him, otherwise the weight of his wet hair would pull him under!"

"Tomorrow let's take a hike and see what's around here," said Rose. "Sounds like fun to me," from Carnelia. After breakfast, Rose and Carnelia started on their trek. The ferry was waiting at the docks and they boarded and crossed the river to Polruan and looked about, returning on the next run to Fowey. John suggested a boat trip to Pridmouth with its Menabilly Grotto, formed from the pushed-up Cornish minerals in the earth. There were half a dozen little villages along the river that they could explore.

One day, they went to Truro to see the new Cathedral being built on the site of old St. Mary's, a 16th century Perpendicular structure. It seemed to be going very slowly; "at this rate maybe it would be finished by 1900." "More likely 1950," answered one of the masons working close by them.

"Father, there is a huge manor in Fowey on a hill above an old church. What is it?"

"It's Place House, the ancestral home of the Treffrys, but very private," he answered.

The days flowed into weeks -- the time went flying. They had covered the area pretty thoroughly going to Par, Polkerris and down to Frenchman's Creek. Tomorrow they would return to Polkerris where there was a restaurant on the Channel that belonged to the Rashleighs of Throwleigh, who also owned Menabilly House. Restormal Castle was not too far away, it had figured heavily in the Civil War between 1642 and 1649 (Cornwall, itself was a 'hot-bed' in the Cromwell days); then to Tywardreath, St. Austell and many more villages. It was August now and time to wind their way back to London.

Returning to Hampstead, they all decided there was no place like home! Barnabus was going to have a heart attack if he didn't calm down... so happy was he to see them. Cat could take them or leave them. Begonia was happy to get back to her pots and pans. She didn't regret a return from holiday -- 'though she saw many things she would never again get a chance at.

The housekeeper had been home with her family in Guildford and was well rested. Rose got back to her music, practicing as though she were trying to make up for all the hours she had missed. She found on the letter tray a request to play at the Wallace Collection of Art. It had arrived yesterday, so she had time to study the matter. The Wallace building had been built by the 4th Duke of Manchester in 1776... later becoming the Spanish Embassy, but now passed into the hands of Richard Wallace to house his father's art collection. There would be a large reception after the concert at which most of the Royalty would be present. Rose guessed this was some of Sullivan's ideas. John

and Carnelia urged her to accept it; so she wrote a note
to the Wallace Committee. She wasn't sure if it was a
paying job or not... but at least it gave her an audience.
Her repertory was considered and she decided on the
piano arrangement of the *21st Concerto* of Mozart to
start with, then some Chopin to follow. August 15th
came and she was well prepared and looked lovely.
She was presented an envelope containing a thousand
pounds.

Tomorrow she'd have to talk to Father about the
Emperor's necklace. It haunted her. Only yesterday
she saw some children grubbing in trash cans, looking
for food. "My dear Rose, you cannot save the world
from starving," her father reminded her on so many
occasions. "But, Father, if I could save *one* I'd be happy. Do you remember what one little girl's life, saved,
meant to *you* when that big dog rescued her that
night?" John Edleigh put his arms around his sweet
daughter and hugged her. "We'll see about something
tomorrow. But we must get back to Bayreuth. Where
is all this struggle with music leading you, Rose? Do
you really want a concert artist's life -- traveling from
city to city the rest of your life!"

"Father, I guess this is a good time to talk: I
believe the Creator-God gave certain people specific
talents -- some to cure; some to preach; some to work
in marble; some to parenthood; and some to soften the
cares of people's lives through song... and I feel strongly
that this is *my* destiny. I cannot forsake it. My practice
is my prayer time -- my performance is the answer to
my petitions. I do not *worship* music, but know there is
a reason for it in my life. I love Jesus Christ above all
things. Will you forgive me that I have failed your
dreams of seeing your house filled with grandchildren?"

"What can a father say after a declaration like that... my heart is filled with pride for your stand!"

146

CHAPTER 15

Back To Bayreuth

Rose would be 39 by the time they saw her again. She arrived in Bayreuth and Liszt greeted her at the railroad station. He didn't look well. "You are radiant, my child," everyone seemed to address her that way -- she was almost middle aged.

"I know *I* look ancient, but I'm very anxious about my son-in-law and friend Wagner. He hasn't been well lately. He has just finished a new opera, *Parsifal*, written about an old German legend of a religious character. He has gone to Venice, which I advised him against, owing to the climate and his health.

"Well, now, Sullivan wrote me from London of your overwhelming success at the Wallace Gallery. I can get you a series of tours in Germany, Austria and France, if you want them."

"I do, Maestro. I want to be busy. I've had a long vacation and it made me more certain that that was what I needed," said Rose.

"We will talk the day after tomorrow -- I want to see what shape you're in," he replied. They parted at her residence.

Rose dreamed that night -- a long persistent, recurring dream. There was a child reaching in a garbage can and she pulled out a toy piano that somebody had discarded. The little girl sat on the curb playing with the keys. Someone passed by and threw down a half eaten loaf and she grabbed it and the toy and fled. Then Rose could sleep no more that night. She felt there was someone calling out to her... so she slipped to her knees and prayed for an explanation of the dream. Returning to her bed, she turned it all over to the Lord.

The next day was spent unpacking and settling in. Her music lay heaviest on her mind; she must deserve the faith Liszt had placed in her. So two hours of Bach and exercising with scales and arpeggios!

On the following day when she neared Liszt's home she had a very queer feeling -- she had caught the glimpse of a child's skirt as she ran and hid behind a pile of debris that was piled up for the sanitation men to clear. Rose walked faster, breaking into a run in pursuit of the child. She called out to her, "Please wait for me -- I want to help you." The child kept running, but Rose ran faster and grabbed her dress and held her. "Where do you live, child... why aren't you in school?" Now the girl knew she was in trouble, for skipping classes was punishable. "Please, lady, I'm very hungry."

"Where is your mother, dear?"

"They put her in the ground last week," and she began to sob.

"Come with me. God has sent me here to find

you. This must be what my dream meant. I am going to take you for some food and then you must wait until I tell my teacher I can't come to my lesson this morning."

The child ate like a starved dog, licking the plate when she finished. Rose pulled back her matted hair and saw a lovely face with tilted nose and big blue eyes. "Will you go home with me, I have a large room and you can sleep and sleep."

Franz Liszt applauded the angelic heart that Rose possessed. "This is going to be an encumbrance to you. You must see that the authorities are notified. Clean her up, I'll pay for the dress and shoes."

He asked her what her name was and her age. The dirty little urchin responded to his kind face and voice and answered, "I am Isobel Bruch, I'm eight years old." Rose was so glad she had studied German.

"Maestro, when Isobel has had a chance to rest and a few good meals, we will talk again about your suggestion. I hope I have not thrown your morning off schedule."

"Not at all when a human life is concerned. We will get started back on lessons next week. Good-bye."

Rose took Isobel's hand and they walked to her residence. "Isobel, wouldn't you like to have a warm bath, then get in my spare bed and sleep. I am going out to buy you some new clothes."

"You are a nice lady, what do I call you?"

"Oh, forgive me, I haven't even introduced myself. I am Rose Edleigh -- I have a mother and father in England -- and a big dog named Barnabus. You would love him." As she combed the girl's hair, she realized what a beautiful child she was.

When Rose left her apartment she asked the

landlady to watch that the girl did not leave. The pro-
prietress immediately said, "You know I'll have to go up
on your rent for the extra one." "That's quite all right --
you should," answered Rose.

The dress was blue with a trim on the collar and
cuffs. She wasn't sure of the shoe size, but the manager
of the store said not to worry, she could bring Isobel in
for a fitting. When Rose entered her place, she saw
Isobel fast asleep... like a little angel. She didn't want
to awaken her, but she had to get her to eat supper.
Upon awakening, Isobel started to run like a frightened
animal, but Rose's voice calmed her, "Isobel, I dreamed
about you the other night... I took it as an omen when I
found you. Do you know about God?" "O yes, my
mama was so good -- she read me the Bible."

"I never knew *my* real mother. She died when I
was born. But I had a nanny who was so kind and
wonderful to me -- she gave me my first piano lessons,"
Rose told her.

"My mother played piano, too. But they took it
away. Then she got sick and couldn't pay a doctor --
she died. I'd like to go to her grave some time."

"Did they just leave you alone in the house?"

"No, I ran away -- I knew they'd take me to a
terrible place in a dark factory. I slept in sheds at night
-- and it was so frightening."

"Would you want to live with me, Isobel? We
could work out something. You would help me with
my chores and I'd teach you your lessons."

"Yes, oh yes," said the child as Rose pulled the
new dress over her head and smoothed it in place.

"It's beautiful, I've never had anything like this... I
wish Mama could see it."

"I sorta' feel that she knows. It was a gift from

Herr Liszt. You see there are many good people in the world. I have some dresses that I could cut down for you. Your jobs will be to wash all the dishes and sweep, then study your lessons I assign. I'll get to the sewing after an hour of piano practice."

"Where are the cleaning things and I can get started," said Isobel. And you would have thought there'd be no nap left on the rugs, she worked so hard. The dishes gleamed when she finished them.

"Can you read?" "Yes", answered the girl, "I was the best in the class."

"Do you know where your text books are?" "Yes, but I'm afraid to go back there."

"Then I'll return to your old place and ask the landlady for them. She will want back rent money, but I'll pay her. After I've heard you read to me, I'll know what level you should be in. I can teach you arithmetic without a book."

"Rose, I am so happy, why are you good to me?"

"Because I was lonely and really didn't know what was missing in my life. So God sent you to me."

"Well, why doesn't He send more children to people like you?," asked the child.

"Perhaps no one prays for them. I'm going to write my father for advice about how I can keep you, and what kind of papers we need when we go to England." Rose decided not to wait on a letter and sent a wireless to Hampstead, it said: "Father, can you come - - need advice badly -- Rose." She knew that would get a quick response.

In three days Mr. Edleigh knocked on Rose's door. It was opened by a small girl with long brown curls. The landlady came running behind him. She could speak English and offered to interpret their conversation. "Excellent," said John. "Oh, have I made a mistake -- I was looking for Miss Rose Edleigh."

"She's at Herr Liszt's house and will be home at five o'clock. Are you Miss Rose's father? I will make you some tea." He sat perplexed, she must be one of Rose's pupils... or does she have something to do with Rose's 'S.O.S.' "Young lady, what is your name?"

"I am Isobel Bruch. Your daughter found me on the street and I was hungry; she took me to get food and is making me these pretty dresses."

Rose entered her residence promptly at five; she rushed into her father's arms.

"Well, Rose, will you do some quick explaining."

"I'll get around to it all after a while. Right now I want to find out all the legalities in having this child live with me -- she's an orphan -- and how to get papers for her to travel with me when I go on tour. Didn't I write you that Liszt has signed me on for piano concerts in Vienna, Hamburg, Paris and Strassburg?"

"When do you start the tour, and how long will you be away?" asked her father.

"December first. The last appearance is on the nineteenth of that month. Then I will be wanting to spend Christmas at home and take Isobel with me. Can it be arranged? If there are any snags, I'll just go to the Emperor myself and give him back his old necklace," pouted Rose.

Rose and Isobel got busy with fixing supper for three. There were chops, fresh asparagus and rice... with gingersnaps for dessert. "Father, you can have my bed and Isobel and I will share the other one. Will you stay *here*... please!"

"Yes, there is so much to discuss and I can't be gone from London very long."

Before retiring, Isobel read to them -- John not understanding a word of the German language, but Rose translated as they went along. Then after playing *Berceuse* on the piano, Isobel said good night to them. "Now, Rose, I want you to wake me early in the morning so I can get started. First I'll go to the British Consulate."

Rose prepared breakfast, Isobel cleaned up the dishes and Mr. Edleigh left for the Consulate. Rose made out problems for Isobel's assignment -- some of them very difficult -- that she was to do while Rose practiced. John Edleigh shook his head in unbelief when he thought of his daughter's quirks... first it was Barnabus I, then Barnabus II, followed by Cat... now a little German waif! She was winsome though, he conceded. And we do have all that room at Hampstead. What would Carnelia think about it; she generally went along with everything that made others happy. He had obtained all the information from Isobel that she could remember about her parents: where and when she was born; her mother's full name; but not much of her father. Then he thought of the school she had attended, they might have a copy of her birth certificate. He leaned over and made some communication with his driver to turn back to the address where the child had lived and find the nearest school. He hit the jack pot the first thing. The teacher wasn't very cooperative until he mentioned his daughter's name and that she planned to go to the Emperor himself! Then all he was looking for came to light. He could carry that data to the passport authorities -- the passport for Isobel would give him more time to research the matter... and also a trial period to see if they were all compatible.

He hurried back to Rose's and asked them to

drop everything -- his cab was waiting. They needed Isobel to go with them for her photo for a passport. That would give them more time to learn about adoption, if that's what they all wanted. In the meantime, she could travel with Rose to France on her tour. It would take about three weeks to clear all the paper work on the travel permit. That afternoon the three set out for the cemetery where Isobel's mother was buried. It was in the area allotted to paupers. John Edleigh put a large bouquet of flowers on the dirt mound, but he was more concerned with what was written on the marker. It read: "Maria Bruch... 1851 -- 1881... Wife of Hans Bruch, died 1875."

Isobel could not possibly remember her father, but he asked her if her mother ever spoke to her about his work or how he died. She did not know how he died; he was working in one of the new factories and there was an accident. Then Mr. Edleigh remembered how it was at that time: Bismarck was having difficulty with the Catholic faction that called itself the "Center." Germany was Protestant; Bismarck was strongly anti-Pope. The Chancellor passed stiff laws against the Catholics for the purpose of bringing the clergy under the control of the State. This was Bismarck's mistake: he didn't know that persecution of the church only made Catholics stronger. Strengthened thus, it caused the Catholic Party to be the strongest political body in the Reichstag. When prosperity came with the Industrial Revolution, a great change took place. The workers began to feel abuse from the demands of the wealthy factory owners. That's when socialistic ideas sprang up -- and it was about this time that Isobel's father fell victim to perhaps 'a convenient accident.' The Socialist Democratic party grew so rapidly that Bismarck was alarmed -- he dropped his animosity against the Catholic "Center," because now he wished their help to crush this enemy, Socialism, which was against his plans for the Empire.

Oh well, that's in the past now -- what we have present is this eight-year-old. He rather liked the child and adoption appealed to him -- but Carnelia's ideas on the matter came first.

It was well that they did not know that in five years William I, King of Prussia -- now Emperor of Germany would be gone -- and Bismarck too -- and that Frederick III would marry Victoria's daughter, Victoria, and they'd give birth to a cocky little 'Kaiser

Bill' who, in thirty-five years from now would cause many parts of Western Europe to lie in a scorching path of destruction.

John Edleigh left the next morning and Rose and Isobel took up their daily schedule. The child was handy about helping Rose in the apartment... then doing her lesson assignments. The principal at Isobel's old school thought it best to let things run on as they were until the Englishman worked out plans with the Consulate -- especially since his daughter had entree with the Emperor of Germany!

Liszt found Rose's lesson prepared as usual... no slackening in proficiency due to the coming of the child into her life. "Maestro, my father is securing a travel permit for Isobel, if you think it would be right for her to accompany me, I will pay for her fare and food -- she is very industrious and helpful to me... besides I hate to interrupt her school assignments."

He thought well of the idea, settling back to discuss her program selections. "Now, for the opening number you will do the *Partita II in C Minor* of Bach -- all six movements, then the *Scherzo in E Flat Minor* by Brahms and last a group of your own romantic compositions. I'd suggest the "Arabesque," the "Emperor's Necklace," and end with "Sad Song." German audiences like those types of music. We have almost two months of intensive work before December first. What will the little girl need in warm clothing?"

"No, Maestro, I cannot let you do that, I have an ample allowance from both my parents, but thank you very much for offering." Time passed so quickly... Isobel was picking up the English language. Rose drilled her all through their meals and bought her text books on English. They were like two sisters. "What will happen if I can't get papers?" asked Isobel. "I'll just steal you and we'll fly to England on a dragon's back!" teased Rose, which made the child squeal with delight. "Don't worry, my father can get what he sets out for -- and if not... I told you about that stinky old priceless necklace!"

So Rose sat at the keyboard for three hours while Isobel did her lessons. At dinner the older one said that tomorrow they would buy her a warm winter coat. "Tomorrow is my birthday; I will be nine years old."

"Well, we will make a party of it... after shopping we'll take lunch at a nice restaurant, then we'll take flowers to your mother's grave. We'll sit and talk to her and tell her what a good girl you are, and how much happiness you've brought to me."

The cab put them out at a department store. "You will also need winter shoes." With shopping over, they splurged on a delicious *mittagessen*. "Say 'lunch', Isobel. Now what am I saying, 'have you ice cream'?" Isobel closed her eyes as she thought: *"Haben sie eis?"*

"Oh, darling, that's wonderful. Now this: 'Have you any food ready'?" The little eyes closed again and she translated it to German... *"Haben sie etwas fertig?"*

"Yes, that's right. You're going to be quite good by the time you go to England with me after the concert tour. Bet you've never been to France." *"Nein...* I mean *no,"* said the student, changing to English.

"Well, that's enough for today. Let's go see your mother now." It was within walking distance, and how bracing the cool air was. "Almost time to wear that new coat," said Rose, as she was buying a bouquet of late blooming flowers from the street vendor. She trimmed around the border and threw out Father's dead plants.

"My mother is happy now. God has told her
about you -- I know He has!"
"You're going to be very tired tonight and we
both have a lot of studying to do. So let's hail a cab for
home."

CHAPTER 16

England -- 1883

Mr. Edleigh had returned to England, Carnelia was full of questions. What's she like? You talk of adoption -- could I be with the child a while before making a decision?"

"Well, you know... you've an advantage over most prospective mothers: they don't know what they are going to be faced with... they can't choose. Tut, tut, 'Nellie', I'm just teasing you. Of course, if it's possible to get her out of Germany she will visit us with Rose for the Christmas holidays. Rose is set on being with this little girl. We're so fortunate, dear, we have one another, a beautiful concert pianist as a daughter, and well situated to care for another little person, don't you think?"

"My dear John, anything you want, so do I."

At tea time Barnabus came out to the lawn -- there wouldn't be many more days they could sit outside. The dog had something in his mouth that trailed behind him. "Would you look at that! What does he want with a leash?" said John as he tried to hook it on Barn's collar. But he'd have nothing of that. He jerked from John's grasp and went running to the back of the yard. He soon returned dragging Cat by the nape of his neck and plunked him at John's feet. "Well, that's the first time I've seen him in several days -- he's been gone while you were away. You know, I believe Barn wants us to put Cat on the leash so he can take him for a walk!" said Carnelia.

They had there own little comedy -- Cat didn't resent the leash and Barnabus went strutting around the yard guiding him until they both grew weary and flopped on the ground together. Carnelia went over to release the cat.

"The du Mauriers had a new baby while you were gone -- Emma is fine. Oh, I saved the *Punch* for you. One of George's illustrations made Parliament sit up and take notice! He is really taking the London reader by storm!"

During the night he could keep remembering Rose saying, "If I could just save *one*," after his remark that she couldn't save *all* the poor. He knew in his heart that the world around him could come tumbling down, but Rose's courage would still keep her waving her little banner.

Bayreuth, November 1883

Liszt could not accompany Rose and Isobel to Hamburg. He reassured her that an agent from the Concert Series Committee would take care of all the arrangements and put her on the train for Vienna; the other two cities would do the same.

"I will have Isobel with me, as her passport is in order."

"She can travel as a companion," said her teacher. Hamburg was a tremendous city, and had it not been for the style of architecture would have looked like Venice -- with all its canal system. The ground was so marshy that buildings had to be built on piles. It took 4,000 piles to support the Rathaus.

Rose and Isobel stayed in a pretty hotel close to the Karl-Muck-Platz. The next evening the two were picked up and taken to the concert hall; it was already filled by the time they arrived at the stage door. At eight o'clock the curtain arose and the tremendous piano stood on the center of the floor surrounded by ferns and different plants. She had been there that morning to get used to the keyboard action. Her mind was on what Liszt had said to her, "Every artist or genius breathes into his work an idea which speaks to our own feelings even before it can be defined." She closed her eyes briefly, reassured herself with, "I am in your hands, Lord, as always." Then striding out swiftly, bowing low to the sea of faces, acknowledged their applause. She sat down confidently. Her deftness and mastery of the ivories was immediately apparent to the audience... so they sat back relaxed to hear her program. The artist on the stage can feel the pulse of the concert hall that can be like a wild lion ready and waiting for the first weakness; and if and when that happens, they are ready to turn on the performer... walk out... or go to sleep! None of that occurred. Her rapport was established and dramatic with them! The *Partita* went off in excellent form -- especially did she love the listeners when she reached the slow movement, and they 'purred'.

Rose sent the write-up from the Hamburg paper to Hampstead for the family, to whom it was no novelty any more, what with all her successes in the past. After a late supper she and Isobel retired for the night. It would be a long day tomorrow. The distance from Hamburg to Vienna was about 675 kilometers. Their train would leave early and they would take a compartment so they could get a good rest; the Vienna audience would be the toughest.

Both slept and dreamed of beautiful scenes that they'd viewed from their windows. Rose had lowered her shade, though, when they almost reached Berlin: memories were still too strong, fortunately it was almost dark. From here on to Prague would be 200 kilometers and by breakfast they'd be seeing the most wonderful sights. At the Czechoslovakian border they entered Austria at Gmund, on the old trading route from Nürnberg to Venice. Both went to the vestibule of the train to look at the strange old walled city. Rose wished they could stop for a while to stroll the streets -- they could see parts of two castles. One had crenelated towers and made her think of Shakespeare's medieval setting of the fourteenth century Verona, Italy, where Romeo and Juliet lived. "Have you ever heard that story, Isobel? If not, we shall read it after the Vienna concert."

They looked down at the valley beyond -- it seemed like a bottomless ravine. Then the train started up and the trees went flying by. It wasn't long before the conductor was announcing Zwettl. There is supposed to be a good abbey here, she had seen pictures of it with the beautiful statues; carved angels seemed to be just hovering overhead.

The tracks were following the Danube River now and the child looked up suddenly and asked, "What is that up on the hill?"

"Well, I know that one quite well" -- then she stopped -- she wanted to shift to another subject... but Isobel looked at Rose and said hesitantly, "What's the matter... is it a bad place?"

"Oh, no, darling. It's just that it reminds me so much of a person I loved and who was going to be a great architect. He came here to study Melk Abbey, and showed me many sketches of it, and told me all about it. It was once a Roman stronghold, but Rome collapsed in the six hundreds. This is Bavarian Country and the Prince of Babenberg built his castle on this cliff-top in the eleventh century -- do you know what a century is? It's the hundred years that follow 101, 201, or 301, etc. The Babenbergs gave up their castle to the Benedictines, who turned it into an abbey. Later the Turks invaded lower Austria and spread ruin everywhere they could. Melk Abbey was gutted by fire but was completely rebuilt in the seventeen hundreds just as you see it now. I promise you that we will come back someday and stay as long as we like!"

"But I must learn a whole lot before I understand

all you're talking about," said Isobel.

From here on they passed hills, meadows, then suddenly rocky gorges and bare cliffs. St. Pölten came into view and only a few miles farther they entered the Wienerwald, the woods that joined Vienna. "Some day soon I'll tell you the story of *Mayerling* that involved Franz Josef's son and his sweetheart, and Beethoven's long walks from Vienna to the Wienerwald for inspiration on his magnificent symphonies. But now let's gather our things together for we are almost in the city. There was an agent waiting for them at the station to take them to their hotel. The ride through the streets was delightful; never had Rose seen such wonders. There was St. Stephen's Cathedral with its belfry rising like an arrow into the sky, a height of 450 feet. It, like St. Paul's in London, had had its troubles -- starting in the mid 12th century, followed by another basilica that was ravaged a century later. Then the 14th century saw its replacement by a Gothic edifice that was damaged by the Turks around the late 17th century. The driver pointed out to them that there were many sculpturings on the south side of the chancel, but the oldest one was the one known as the 'Christ with the toothache.'

Just before reaching the Staatsoper (opera house), they passed the Lobkowitz Palace, built in 1685. It was here in the Erocia Saal that Beethoven presented the *Eroica Symphony*, in 1804, for the first time. The cab stopped in front of the hotel where she was met by the music committee.

"And who is the one with you?" one asked. "She is one of my students," said Rose without going into details.

"We will dine in tonight and in the morning I will go to the opera house and practice the piano. Are you afraid to stay alone and study your assignments?"

"No, I've never felt so safe in my life -- I was always scared until you came along," and the child hugged her tightly.

Rose was beginning to feel like a traveling carnival by now. Isobel got out her lesson assignment and started her English vocabulary first. "I'll leave you for a while to go to the Staatsoper to run over a few pieces. She toyed with the idea of an unprecedented thing: to play something to break the ice. She had labored over her own paraphrase of *Tales of the Vienna Woods*... with many difficult cadenzas -- but then thought better of the idea, and decided if an encore were needed, to do it then.

She walked the three blocks back to their hotel to get Isobel and find a cozy sidewalk cafe. The child needed fresh air and exercise. There was one close to the opera house in a little park, so they started for that. Rose looked up from her newspaper and saw this figure cartwheeling across the grass and when the acrobat stopped she saw it was her own Isobel. "Why, girl, haven't you told me about your gymnastic skill? Where did you learn to do all that?"

"My mother played piano for a dancing class and I was allowed to participate with the other girls. Then Mama got real sick and had to quit, so did I, also."

"Well, we must do something about this wasted talent of yours... soon as we get back to Bayreuth. Let's go now, after a light supper then off to the concert."

At eight o'clock the Staatsoper was filled... all but the Emperor's box. Then a hush fell over the hall. Franz Josef and Empress Elizabeth entered their stall and stood briefly while the audience paid respect to his presence. Shortly the curtain went up -- and it was like

Hamburg all over again -- except after Rose sat down for the *Partita*, she suddenly got up and went to the footlights and said she felt she must start with a number she had not listed on the program, because of her over-whelming joy of the beauty of Austria. And she started again... *Tales of the Vienna Woods*. She played with such gusto in one moment, shifting to a romantic pathos the next, that the Vienna audience fell in love with her. One could hear a sigh from the listeners as she concluded the variations. Then the program took its regular course.

When she came out for her curtain call, the Emperor stood in his box and bowed to her. She returned his gesture with such appreciation that she almost forgot to resume her upright position.

Well, Vienna was over. But what to do with all those flowers. She decided to take them to the charity hospital on her way to her hotel. Next morning they'd board the train again -- for Salzburg, some 350 or more kilometers. By leaving Vienna early they would reach their destination by nightfall. Rose looked at her Austrian map and saw they'd follow the Danube River to Krems, Dürnstein, Weissenkirchen, Spitz and back to Melk... from there to Grein, St. Florian, and continuing west they'd be in Salzburg. She would have loved to stop the train and walk through those wooded yew trees, splash in the streams... but remembered how cold it would be, for it was nearing mid-December. Except for the yew trees all was covered with snow, a few glistened with icicles. There would be an occasional ski-slope with sportsmen flying down the hillsides. The Abbey at Krems was visible from the train. "Oh, Isobel, if we could only take a little peek into it -- Fritz told me so much about it... he would say that the painters and sculptors, working with the great architects, possessed attributes which in the sister art of music produce the equivalence of a Mozart or a Haydn. Soon we will be in Dürnstein. Oh, look over there... can you see it on top of that rocky ridge... that's Dürnstein. We had a King in England long ago, about 700 years really, named Richard the Lionheart. He left England to go on a crusade to the Holy Land. The purpose was to insure the safety of the pilgrims to Jerusalem, and to recover the Holy Land for Christianity. There were seven Crusades made -- but the Lionheart went on the third one, which was not altogether for holy purposes. The King of England, France and Germany were in on this one -- and Acre fell after a two-year siege. But on his return home Richard had to pass through Dürnstein, and the Duke of Austria, Leipold V, got even with Richard for the bloody insult the Duke had suffered when the King of England removed the Austrian's banner from the tower in Acre, Palestine, thus humiliating his honor. It so happened that Richard had to cross the Duke's Austria on his way home. He dressed himself up like a peasant, but they still found him out when he was spending the night at Dürnstein. He was arrested and locked up in a fortress. A year later Blondel found the King by going from castle to castle with his stringed instrument and singing songs that he and his master had composed together. Finally, the musician came across the courtyard of a prison at Dürnstein and when King Richard heard the song he recognized it as the one he and Blondel had written. He answered his minstrel by singing the second verse. He was finally freed, but it cost England a tremendous ransom!"

Next the train stopped at Weissenkirchen, only to take on a passenger. And off they started again. Rose and Isobel ate their lunch that the hotel in Vienna had packed -- soon Isobel fell into a drowsy state and slept through Spitz, Melk, Grein and Mauthausen while Rose contemplated on many things. She wondered if this was truly what her life was supposed to be: a link connecting an old generation to a new one by passing on what they had acquired, and finally giving it all back to the Creator in a sterling condition. Was this the meaning of the Parable of the Talents in the Book of Matthew? She, too, became drowsy and joined Isobel in the land beyond consciousness. The train gave a jolt when it stopped in Linz, a town that straddled the Danube River, and the two awoke. They were more than halfway to Salzburg. "Don't you think you should start your lesson study now? Your long-division is getting so good that soon we will be getting on to square roots: that's when any number multiplied by itself gives a total sum. But to get the square root of any total sum takes a certain arithmetic formula. I think it's the most fun of any math function. Why don't you practice on English phrases that you can use when we get to London for Christmas. So Isobel dug in, while Rose took out her dummy keyboard and did scales and chords. After Salzburg, and the last one in Paris, they would get a train to Calais. A ferry crossing on the English Channel could be exciting, landing at Dover, where her father would join them for London.

As the train neared Salzburg, the outline of the Hohensalzburg -- a great fortress of the Prince-Archbishops -- loomed up on the horizon. This city was the birthplace of the musician W. Amadeus Mozart.

It was time to gather their belongings and get off for the station. They were again met and escorted to a hotel by a tour manager. Tonight a good rest would be needed for the next day's musical. Isobel was showing signs of fatigue, and Rose, herself, felt that this was getting to be a bit much! Supper was brought to their room and they slept almost 'til noon the next day. Rose suggested a cab for a drive to the Mozarteum so she could see the piano, and then drive through the city to look at the beautiful buildings. The driver took them to the Domplatz, the fine city square with its Cathedral and ecclesiastical palaces, Mirabell Gardens, Church of St. George, and St. Peter's Church.

Isobel stammered to the cabbie, "Could we see Mozart's birthplace?" He found it for them at #9 Getreidegasse, and pointed up to the third floor where the musician lived for about seventeen years. He thought the child would like to see the Glockenspiel on the east side of the Residenz, so he took them there. When Rose started to pay... he said, "No charge for the Glockenspiel, that part was on me."

The concert that night was well received, with several curtain calls. For an encore she did a humorous paraphrase on a simple Mozart tune... with lots of embellishments. The audience went wild with delight.

"One more, Isobel, and then we head for a wonderful place: home!"

Paris was just too tiring! Rose did what she came for and that's about all. She cabled her father just when to meet them at Dover. Paris had been a letdown, perhaps because she expected it to top what they had already seen. She found it vulgar. Just too blasé, she reckoned... and besides she couldn't understand a word those Frenchmen spoke!

After two weeks on the road their clothes were beginning to look a bit shabby. Rose just wanted to get home! She decided to leave a few things in a rented space at the depot: her keyboard and Isobel's books. They could manage getting on the ferry and sit back and breathe the fresh air. "You're going to love Hampstead Heath. It won't be at its best this time of the year, but the open fire, the rides through the light snow will be great... Can you ride a horse?"

"Oh, no, I'd be afraid to -- but I want to see your Barnabus and Cat. I had a cat once... but Mama said she was killed by the rats."

They could see the shiny cliffs of Dover rising above the water's edge -- the child wondered why they were so white. "Oh, Isobel, almost the entire history of England began here -- everyone visiting the country should enter it just as we are now. Close your eyes a minute. This is our first history lesson on England. Imagine we are two humans that lived 9,000 years ago, before our Lord was born. We are wearing skins of animals and equipped with weapons hewn from stone secured to a wooden pole by twisted cords of hemp. We may have come from as far as Asia, or maybe just France (or whatever it was called then). We're hunters and looking for new findings farther west -- our old tribesmen spoke of the weather being warmer and the hunting better. So one day we ventured toward the sun and followed it westward. We tramped over ice and hard-packed snow for days and days... maybe several months. And one night when the moon was full and the 'hooties' were restless we heard an earth-crushing sound -- a fearful noise and it echoed and reverberated -- we knew not what to think and slunk back under the snow, pulling our dogs close to us in fright. We lay in frozen fear until day brightened. Then we set out, retracing our steps eastward to find the source of the catastrophic blast of the night before. Soon we came to an abrupt break in the earth's crust that went down, down like a straight wall... and straining our eyes, we could see a stream of water with ice floes rushing downward. We stood like dumb animals. How could we get back to our homelands? We existed the best we could. You were the mama and I was the papa... we killed animals for our food and lit fires with pieces of flint. We later had families and they pushed on farther westward; their families in turn gradually became used to their new world, learning to carve and decorate their stone. There came a rise in the sea level brought on by the icecap melting -- and what we call Britain was cut off completely from Europe... and that's the Channel that we have just crossed. That Age of Man was followed by the Neolithic Period that lasted 2,000 years. In that time crude farming implements were being made and improved on. This progress went on until about the Iron Age, 600 B.C. And then we come to the Romans... we'll talk about them later. OK, let's get our things together, we get off this big 'iron horse' which, incidentally, was not built in the Iron Age... nor by the Trojans... we'll get to them later, too.

"Hurry, Isobel, I think I see Father -- that tallest fellow at the gate," but it seemed like forever weaving through the crowds, knocked about, dropping parcels. Finally, Rose was in father's arms, and little Isobel was entwined with them.

Mr. Edleigh said, "I already have our tickets for the next train to London. Our stableman will pick us up at Waterloo station and take us out to Hampstead."

CHAPTER 17

Christmas at Hampstead

Hampstead was draped in icicles and the ground was white all about. Father had something up his sleeve that was driving him crazy, but he wanted so very much for it to be a surprise... so he kept biting his tongue. It had been a long hard day for the two travelers, and Carnelia thought they ought to be packed off to bed immediately. "Breakfast at eight, and we'll talk our heads off then."

Isobel's room was the prettiest thing she ever saw -- all done in pink and lavender. There was a four-poster bed with a lace 'roof' on top of it. Rose told her it was a tester bed. "Am I to sleep in it all by myself?"

"Yes, it's yours, and it will always be yours, and when Father fixes things up with the adoption agencies we're all going to be so happy together. Isobel, I want you to try real hard to speak in English. Tomorrow we will learn some English phrases pertaining to the Christmas season. Good night, dearest child, you've been a marvelous little companion. Before your prayers let's start the Book of Mark. You read the first five verses in your German copy and I will re-read them in English and tomorrow you translate them on your own. That's the only study work you will do during the holidays." Isobel clung to Rose and said, "I love you, Rose," in perfect English. And the candle was blown out.

The next morning Father could at last quit 'biting his tongue.' "Wait 'til you see what's in the stables!"

"Now, John, let's finish eating and get on some warm clothing first," begged Carnelia.

In the stable were two of the most beautiful quarter-horses that Rose had ever seen. She stood petrified, gazing at them. Carnelia laughed and said that John had been waiting for an excuse to buy them.

"They are your Christmas gifts... yours and Isobel's."

"Oh, Father, that's the nicest thing in the world. I will teach Isobel to ride before we leave the last of December."

"Now let's go inside and hear all about your concert tour." The fire was crackling in the drawing room. Carnelia was beginning to decorate for the Yule Season.

"Vienna was the best, I believe. The Emperor and Empress Elizabeth were there. You remember, hers was the home we saw at Possenhofen the year we went to Bavaria. At Vienna I did something daring: I opened my program with my paraphrase on *Tales From the Vienna Woods* -- and the Emperor acknowledged it! I didn't care for Paris. But let's don't talk shop any more. I want to know what's been going on here. How is the Reverend Aston, and the du Mauriers, and all the old neighbors? Can we have them over for Christmas afternoon?"

"Indeed we will, Cook is preparing sweets now for the occasion," said Carnelia.

"Now, Father, can we get down to some serious talk: I have a plan, but I know nothing about getting it started. It's the necklace that the German Emperor gave to me -- will you have it evaluated by a man who knows his business. If it is worth enough I can add that to my concert tour pay, and maybe that will buy a little piece of land in Bayreuth. I can get a home started for young 'street children.' Father, this is very important to me. Perhaps it will take several years to happen, but I'm obsessed with the project. It will be located at the place where I found Isobel and I'll name it for her mother. I want Isobel to be trained to be the directress. She wants it too. I know I ask too much of you but I also know the pleasure you get from granting my requests. I promise I will make you proud of my music someday."

"Why, Rose, stop talking that way -- I think it's the most unselfish, loving thing you can do -- and we'll put this thing over first class. And as for being proud of you, you exceeded my pride long ago."

The next day was not so cold so Rose and Isobel bundled up and ventured to the stable. Hector put the saddles on the new horses and told the ladies to walk around with them for a while and talk to them with little offerings of sugar lumps. When Rose felt the horse could trust her, she mounted her and paced her slowly around the yard. Isobel watched everything she did -- and let out a rigmarole in German to her own horse at which her mentor said, "Isobel, she only understands English. Now tell her what your name is and stroke her on the nose... here's a lump of sugar. That helps to make friends with her."

After an hour or so Isobel put her right foot in the stirrup and threw her other over to mount her trotter. You could almost see the disgust on the beast's face! Such clumsiness, she must have thought. The girl finally maintained her balance, but the horse wouldn't budge. Rose took the reins and led her around the grounds with Isobel astride her.

Carnelia was bringing out a tea tray and all sat on bundles of hay in the stable. "What shall I name her, Rose?" asked Isobel. "That's your decision... she's all yours." The child thought for a while and came up with 'Snitzel.' That's who she is. "Come, 'Snitzel,' get your sugar." And she did. Everybody laughed at her obedience... and from then on Isobel and Snitzel were a pair.

"Let's go in by the fire for a while, you too, Hector. Your tree you selected is perfect and I think we'll start decorating it after dinner," suggested Carnelia. Tomorrow would be Christmas Eve and there was much to do. "The Reverend Aston and his brood would be six, George and Emma du Maurier and their three children, the Haraldsons, and the people next door -- that makes nineteen, counting us, for Christmas afternoon," said Rose.

Barnabus and Cat felt slighted; since that 'foreigner' came they hadn't had their proper place in the household. So they sulked, spending most of their time back of the stable and doing a bit of mischief involving some neighbor's stray ducklings. The Edleighs were notified of the fact... and subtly reminded what guns were for!

Rose was ashamed that she had neglected her old friends... and whistling loudly for them they came running and she tumbled to the ground with them and played their old games with the ball. She introduced Isobel and said to them, "Oh, Barn, we were so unkind -- it was just that Father was so excited about the horses that we didn't want to dampen his spirit. Come in to the fire, but you must behave! Remember that antique of Carnelia's collection that you broke? Well, no more!"

Everybody fell asleep that Christmas Eve night with visions of sugar plums -- 'cause they'd eaten too much! They came marching in with hot tongs and pinchers and danced on the bed covers. "I shan't eat another bite 'til tea-time and maybe not then," moaned Rose.

They had all decided on not buying any gifts this Christmas, but just enjoy the great gift of having each other's love. There would be lots of music and Isobel had made up her own dance to a merry tune that Rose and Carnelia had worked up.

Now it was time for the guests -- the du Mauriers arrived first and all the Edleighs admired the oldest son; Gerald's growth and manliness had developed since Rose saw him last. Then the others trickled in close behind. When all had arrived and their coats were removed, the program started. First they all sang "Joy to the World." That was followed by a request for George du Maurier to sing and play *Der Lieben Langen Tag*. Isobel exclaimed with glee, "I know that one -- it's a German song." He sat at the piano, not a sound was made but that sweet melody floating across the room. Even the fire quit crackling! There was hardly a dry eye in the group. How he could play on their souls with his voice. After a deep sigh from the listeners as the last note died away, the rest of the musical went on. Rose and Carnelia were requested to play their usual "Ave Maria" by Bach. Mr. Edleigh looked about him and wondered if any man ever felt such a richness as this in this temporal life: friends, music, warmth from a glowing fire! He closed his eyes for a moment, and he cried within himself: "I'm not a 'Religious' man, God, but I know You as my Creator -- and the giver of all beauty -- make me a worthy man in Thy sight."

They concluded their singing with "Silent Night," Rose at the piano, Carnelia with violin, George taking the voice lead, and Isobel doing the last verse in its original German. Then Begonia opened the doors to the dining room where a table threatened to collapse with the weight of all the goodies. The children had their separate table to keep them from underfoot of the oldsters.

Barnabus and Cat were permitted in the kitchen; Cat ate daintily and gave Barn a scowl when he started wolfing it down.

When the guests left, the family flopped down to rest. No dinner would be served tonight. John Edleigh stirred up the dying embers of the Yule log and Isobel brought in her King James Version and read the first chapter of Mark in splendid English.

Rose said, "Isobel, you have performed the very best presentation of the day. What *we* all did was native to us -- and *you* have learned to give this beautiful reading in a foreign tongue."

To the stables the next morning with Barnabus and his pouting friend following close behind. Cat sneaked up from the rear and gave a deft leap, landing on Barn's back. He was going to have a trotter, too. The canine gave him a dirty look, but didn't shake him off... They could do that silly riding thing, also.

Snitzel had become docile by now and Isobel mounted her like a real equestrian. Before they left Hampstead she was in love with this England! In three days they were off for Dover again on their way back to Bayreuth. It was the most tearful departure she had ever experienced, but Rose was consoled that her parents loved Isobel, and her father would get down to all the red tape of the adoption.

The return trip was a let-down. Everything was draped in white -- there had been some real hard snow storms since they left Germany. It was New Year's day when Bayreuth was reached... all businesses were closed down. It was good, though, to get back to their old quarters and start work again -- Rose at the piano and Isobel at her lessons. Isobel worried that Snitzel would forget her.

"She won't, dear, and by the time you go back to Hampstead you will have a father and mother all of your own. But you must never forget your *real* mother. We're going to make our dream come true. I left the necklace with Father to be appraised -- and that will be our start. You must soon begin regular school and get your credentials to run the 'Home' for the unfortunate little ones.

Liszt had four paying students for Rose; they were children of nobility, and the tuition would be generous. "I hope you will accept my gift to endow your dreams. You've brought me joy and much purpose to living," said her teacher.

The year 1884 got back on regular schedule. Liszt, in order that Rose kept her goal of founding a Home, had his banker-friend notify her that a trust fund had been set up in the "Maria House Fund." In the spring there would be a good concert tour -- not so demanding in traveling long distances: one in Bayreuth, Frankfurt and Berlin. Until then Rose and Isobel would stay busy. Not long ago, Liszt suffered a terrible shock: his friend who was also his son-in-law, Richard Wagner, died. The entire music world went into mourning for the great man. His health had been bad for four years, which caused him to leave Bayreuth for a better climate in Italy. When the Bavarian King Ludwig II heard of his death in Venice -- he cried, "Frightful, terrible -- his body belongs to me! Bring his coffin to Bayreuth." There his burial took place, laying him to rest in the garden of his old home Wahnfried.

King Ludwig had sponsored Wagner in almost all his musical enterprises -- giving him financial support. When the Bavarian King read of the world's grief, he said, "It was I who saved him for the world and the worlds to come." And it was after Wagner's death, it seemed, the 'Dream King' started falling to pieces. His building schemes were always wild. Not satisfied with his earlier bizarre castle of Neuschwanstein in 1870 he started on Linderhof the same year; he built the Opera House at Bayreuth in 1872; and in 1873 came the acquisition of Herrenchiemsee, rebuilding it in 1878, a year before Linderhof was finished. After Wagner's demise Ludwig was on the verge of madness and declared insane later in 1886. He was found in the waters of Lake Starnberg close to Berg Castle that same year, where he had been confined.

But this was not the norm for musicians -- most led uneventful lives, loving their art and passing it down to a new generation.

A letter arrived from Mr. Edleigh the last of March. All was well at Hampstead; but they were really looking forward to the spring months. They knew that Rose's teacher, Liszt, was saddened by Wagner's death -- "but, my darling daughter, if I could leave behind, after I'm gone, all the beauty that that man has created at God's bidding -- well, it in a way, lessens the pain of that certain 'curtain-call' that we must all face." Then he closed his letter telling about Her Majesty's great trial in the death of her youngest son, the Duke of Albany. He was the intellect of the family, proficient in music and painting, possessed fine judgement, and was loved by all. While visiting in southern France, he had received a severe fall when ascending the stairs. At first it didn't seem serious, but during the night a fit of apoplexy came on him and by three a.m. he had died in the arms of his equerry, Captain Perceval. The letter was signed with four animal paws... which always made Rose smile.

The next week was the first concert of her series in Germany. It was in Bayreuth; she would play the Beethoven *Les Adieux Sonata*, Chopin's *Mazurka*, Op.17, No.4, Bach's *Prelude and Fugue in D* and close with three of her own compositions.

The reviews read: "Her ability to bring forth pure music from the piano was most apparent in the Beethoven Sonata and in Chopin's *Mazurka*, both of which she played euphoniously and poetically. Probably the most outstanding quality of Miss Edleigh's performance is the ease with which she can transcend in one moment from a whispering pianissimo to a powerful thunderous climax in the next. The Chopin was beautiful at all times -- delicately shaded and subtle. Her own innovations in the last group show promise of a new trend -- and a fascinating purity of sound, some in which she explored the use of the whole-tone scale."

Liszt was behind stage and congratulated her over and over again. Rose was glad for him -- for that is what teachers thrive on: hearing their students perform. He seemed to be greying over the trauma of Wagner's sudden death. Next week she would repeat the same program in Frankfurt. Having never been to that city she wanted to read up on it -- and see what kind of audience to expect. The library wasn't too far so she walked there to research. She read that the importance of Frankfurt had always depended on the river crossing. The Celts first drove out the Romans, then the Allemani (ancient Germans) drove the Celts away, later the Franks routed the Allemani, so the place became known in 500 A.D. as the Frank's Ford. It was the ford that made the destiny of Frankfurt because the main route from south to north had to pass through it. Roads meant trade -- which brought about prosperity. Arts and learning follow prosperity, resulting in tolerance and liberalism. There were old documents of a Customs House here as early as 1074 -- and an Imperial mint of Frankfurt in 1194. Since 1240 late summer fairs were held, then in 1330 spring fairs started. Rose would be playing during the spring fair.

She had turned forty, but never stopped long enough to see what it felt like. There were gifts... small things... from Hampstead and a poem that Isobel had written for her.

The train ride to Frankfurt was nice... being only 200 kilometers away they would arrive by dark. With a good night's sleep she'd be in shape for the concert. The papers gave her excellent reviews. One stated: "The artist stood at the full height of her virtuosity -- and the audience begged for numerous encores." Another said, "Played with marvelous clarity and brilliance." And still another, "Technical brilliance and musical instinct. She charms the listener through her rhythmic temperament and beautiful delicacy of touch."

Rose and Isobel slept soundly next morning... their train would not leave until afternoon. Since it was almost 600 kilometers, they would not arrive in Berlin until the next day. The concert engagement was not for two more days so that would give her time to rest and practice. She had dreaded the thought of returning to Berlin. Even after all these years and her successful career... and finding little Isobel... she still had an emptiness in the middle of her heart. Though she thought she carried his spirit with her -- it just wasn't the same as laying her hand on his: the hand of a musician and a brilliant architect. Well, Heaven will keep for us someday, she almost said out loud.

After the cab put them out at the station and their belongings were settled in the compartment, they began to take a look at the wonderful countryside. Rose took out her itinerary; closest town was Bad Hersfeld, next Kassel, Braunschweig, Potsdam then Berlin, having slept through much of it... they arrived in Berlin around noon. Rose said to her young companion -- "How's about me taking a sabbatical next year and just me teaching at our apartment; and you beginning regular school?"

"I'd like that very much."

"Well, that it will be, then. Oh, look, I can see some old ruins of a building that I bet was a monastery. Once the town of Bad Hersfeld must have been famous as a resort. It resembled some scenes from Grimm's fairy tales, remember 'Kinder und Hausmarchen'?"

A vendor came through the aisle with *wurst, gurke, traubensoft* -- Isobel had to translate those: sausage, cucumber, and grapejuice for Rose, as they were not part of her academic vocabulary. The child had taught Rose many everyday idioms.

"Sounds good to me -- let's eat and watch the last rays of the sun going behind that verdant horizon. Is it my time to translate that to *you*," said the elder. Just before dark they pulled into Kassel. There was a wonderful castle here, Löwenburg. Only a vague outline of it was visible. "Some day we will come back and see the Schloss Wilhelmstal, and several more old ones in the area. I remember the legendary castle of the *Sleeping Beauty* -- I think it was called Schloss Sababurg. Yes, indeed, we'll come back!" and she yawned and looked over at the beautiful sleeping child.

The next morning Rose opened her eyes just as the train was pulling out from Braunschweig. She nudged Isobel. "That's not the way we spell 'Brunswick' in England. There is supposed to be a bronze lion standing in the Burgplatz -- it's dated 1166 and it symbolizes Henry the Lion; he had built the city's Romanesque Cathedral." Looking at her watch she couldn't believe it was only five-thirty a.m., and told Isobel to go back to sleep. As for herself she would just lie there and watch the country go by. She had never indulged herself really, in lolling around or being idle, but now it seemed to engulf her and mesmerize her -- she was that wide-eyed girl meeting a young German guide who spoke English with a beautiful accent. He and she had walked hand in hand in the Tiergarten park, sipped tea in the little nature garden near the Brandenburger Tor.

The Berlin concert would be for Fritz... perhaps the good Lord would allow him to hear her.

After lunch -- seem's breakfast got lost somewhere between Isobel's sound slumber and her own nostalgic visit with a memory -- their train pulled into the Berlin station with same old procedure: committee people escorting her to the hotel, and telling her a car would pick her up for the concert hall the next day.

The program went off very well with many curtain calls demanded by the audience. So in the end she came out and announced in German, "This one is for a dearly loved German lad that died a hero's death. It is called 'A Sad Song'."

Now back to Bayreuth to resume a quieter, more studious life. That weekend Liszt asked Rose and Isobel to come to his home... he would send a carriage for them. They were delighted, having heard so much about his villa near Haus Wahnfried, where Wagner and Cosima, Liszt's daughter, lived -- and where the Wagner descendants would always live.

When the hansom drove up to Rose's residence Isobel was peering through the window in eager antici-pation. So off they went. After an early supper all walked to the nearby Haus Wahnfried; Liszt wished to place some roses he had cut from his own garden on Wagner's grave. As they stood by the music-Titan's mound, Liszt said quietly, "I feel as Victor Hugo did: 'We are all under the sentence of death, but we have an interval and then our place knows us no more. Some spend their time in listlessness, some in high passions, but the wisest are the ones who are given to the expression of art in its many forms: music, paint-ing, literature, -- for art comes to you professing frankly to give nothing but the highest quality to your moments as they pass.' The world will know more of Wagner in the years to come than is now known of him. But, Rose, our art is as a gift that we bestow at our Creator's feet."

That evening they listened to some improvisations by her teacher. Plans for the summer were discussed; she told him that her father was coming to Germany to see about the adoption of Isobel... then they would all return to Hampstead Heath for the holidays. Liszt's English was better and Rose's German was much im-proved... mostly because of Isobel's living with her.

"Yes, it is good. The young one will receive her education and come back to Germany to direct the 'Home' we set up. Our account in the bank is growing as word gets around," he said.

Rose observed how often Liszt used the term 'we'... he must have invested quite a sum in it.

At the season's last class recital Rose's students seemed to play with more maturity than those of the other teachers that entered theirs. She was proud of them.

Mr. Edleigh arrived the next week with the good news that Isobel was theirs! All the papers had been in order -- and she need but add 'Edleigh' to her other two names. There was great rejoicing that evening. Reservations were made in a very fine restaurant and 'Miss Isobel Bruch Edleigh' did her own ordering: "Haben sie lammelfleisch? Ich möchtepastoffein, spinat, bitte." Then Mr. Edleigh bravely said, "Ditto, here." The waiter looked puzzled and Rose covered for Father by stating in German what she and he wanted.

"Could you be ready to travel by day after tomorrow?" asked her father.

"Yes, Isobel's school finished last week for their holidays. How wonderful to have a little sister" -- and she looked at Isobel. The child's eyes filled with tears and Rose became alarmed. "Don't you want us for a family?"

"Oh, yes, yes... I am so happy," Isobel stammered. "A home of my own -- with Carnelia, you, Father, Barnabus and Cat."

"I forgot to mention in my last letter that Barn had developed rheumatism -- drags his back leg pretty badly. The Vet had given him some pills for the pain; Cat sits with him licking the bad leg. Those two are 'something' together!" And Isobel's eyes welled up -- but she was too big for that, now that she'd soon be eleven. Rose spoke to her father about the trust fund Liszt was starting for the 'Home' in Bayreuth. Did you find out if the necklace was worth much?"

"Worth *much*! -- Do Kings give fakes?"

"*How* much, Father?"

"Oh, Cartiers appraised it roughly around fifteen thousand pounds. Not to be sniffed at, I'd say, wouldn't you?"

It was the day to leave Bayreuth -- there was so much luggage, it took several porters. When the train started up, they all settled into a quiet little retreat. "You know, Rose, I've been over this rail track so much I'm beginning to feel like an iron horse! Are you going to leave the Royal Academy in London for good?"

"No, Father, just until we get our 'project' going. With my concert tour income and the necklace plus Franz Liszt's trust fund... it won't be long. Then Isobel will be old enough to go back and forth from Bayreuth to London alone -- maybe five years from now."

"But, Rose, I'm getting old, I don't see you much. I will soon retire from the Stock Exchange."

"Oh, Father, you're the youngest man I ever saw with an old-maid daughter of nearly 41!"

The train finally arrived in London and they got a diligence instead of having their own stableman meet them. Walking up the path was Carnelia and the two animals, Barnabus and Cat; old Barn trying to navigate without limping. Isobel got down on the grass and let Cat pounce all around her, while the canine licked her hands and nudged at her neck.

What a homecoming! "Here's your new daughter, Carnelia. Maybe I shouldn't mention this: but under Roman Law -- from which our very own laws derive -- an adopted person has a closer hold on his unnatural parents than a natural born. You cannot disinherit an adopted member." So he teased Rose about behaving herself!

During the summer they took to going into London to show Isobel the sights of her new country. All four of them spent the next Wednesday at the Tower of London, Rose carefully explaining the historic features of it -- talking sometimes in German and other times in English. There was still time to go to Westminister Abbey, after which they dined at the Savoy Hotel.

Most of all, though, Isobel liked best the days they just stayed home and she could be with Snitzel. The horse remembered her. This summer she would teach her to jump over low fences. Gerald du Maurier came over to play lawn tennis -- though their communication in speech was lacking -- they understood what to do with a racket and ball; the 'deuce' was a new word to her, meaning each side had made even points. Isobel was a good player -- in fact she was good at about everything.

Summer was flying by. The family often had tea on Sunday afternoon. Next week Arthur Sullivan would be out at Hampstead to join them, along with the du

Mauriers, the Reverend Mr. Aston and several others. .
Sullivan was looking forward to hearing his former
pupil play. Cook had out-done herself on the sesame
seed cake, raspberry jam, scones and cucumber sand-
wiches. Barn and Cat kept their distance, he was sensi-
tive about his lameness, so Cat hung behind with him.
Du Maurier mentioned Isobel's tennis prowess and she
blushed. "But, Isobel, should you try to make a quarter
horse a race horse? I believe they are mostly for
prancing and jumping -- dress-horses, am I right?"

The Reverend Aston was glad of a chance to talk
with Sullivan about his *Te Deum*, which the Queen
loved more than anything ever written. At dusk they
all went into the drawing room and had music. Rose
and Carnelia surprised Sullivan with a melody of arias
from his opera, *Ivanhoe*. His comment was that if he
could have had Carnelia and Rose on stage it would
have been a success. "By the way, Rose, when are you
returning to the Academy? There is a real need for
you in London."

Rose then told him about Isobel's young childhood -- how she had found her rummaging through
trash cans. At that moment Isobel entered the room...
"See, what a lovely young lady she is? Isobel is one of
the joys of my life. You know about the gift of the
necklace from Emperor Wilhelm... Father had had it
appraised, and a dear sum it came to! So that, plus a
fund from Maestro Liszt and fees for my tour give us a
whopping start toward a 'Foundling Home' (except we
can't call it that... too stigmatic). It will be named for
Isobel's poor dead mother. We shall call it 'Maria
House'. Professionals will run it until Isobel is old
enough and qualified to direct it."

"That is a noble undertaking, my dear. I've al-

ways said that music brings out the best in a person --
which causes me to sermonize on a trend that's creep-
ing in. In the field of painting it's asserting itself in
forms called 'realism'. The devotees of this school
started out by declaring classical art -- the only kind
we've known for hundreds of years -- was deceptive;
merely wishful thinking. To them (the realists) there
was one standard: 'art for art's sake'; morals, ethics, or
romance played no part in it. The new artist considered it his right to paint as he saw... 'behind a subject'
to be depicted. With the lack of discipline in departing
from true perspective -- both in writing and painting --
they slump into decadence. I fear the same might happen in music. Be careful, Rose. The young genius
Debussy has rules in his new form -- but others through
imitation may turn it into 'liberties'. I note that you are
experimenting with what Claude Debussy introduced as
the 'whole-tone scale'. Go easy with the 'new thought'.

"There's Van Gough, the Dutch painter. In 1877
he intended studying for the church. I hear he has
some outlandish canvases in the galleries in London.
He certainly has a flair for violent colors!... Gracious,
the guests have all left and here I sit talking you to
death. I'm sorry."

"Oh, no, Sir Arthur (Queen Victoria had granted
him his title in '83). You make so much sense. We
will get the stable driver to take you back to your quarters if you feel you must leave."

The last of August Rose and Isobel left Hampstead Heath for Bayreuth. The train trips seemed to be
getting longer each time. "I tell you what, Isobel, we'll
hire us a helium balloon next time -- how'd that be?"

"Oh, I don't know... you're just joking, aren't you!"

"Yes, dear. Let's just relax and rest up for all the

work lying ahead."

Eventually, Bayreuth was reached and they went straight to their place. Tomorrow we must clean and go shopping for provisions, thought Rose. Much mail had accumulated in her summer's absence: a letter from Kathryn and William Tilly -- it made her feel good to know how happy they were, living in Berlin and his work going so well with the architectural firm. "I still miss my old buddy Fritz, as I know you do many times more. Perhaps we can get together in the spring. Loving you, Kathryn and William."

"I will tell you about them sometime," Rose told Isobel. "Now, your school starts tomorrow -- are your clothes in order? I must call on Herr Liszt about my schedule... or would you like to go with me?"

"Yes, maybe you've forgotten some of your German -- and I can help with interpretation," as she hugged Rose.

"Uh huh, and we'll see how good you are in your English classes this term," teased her new sister.

They took a nice long walk to Liszt's house. As he was with a student the two waited in the garden. He beamed when he greeted Rose... and the 'Liebling', as he always referred to Isobel.

"My dear, can you handle a few more students? I have been a bit tired lately. I would like to turn them over to you and have more time for my composing. And by the way, I suggested you as soloist for the Philharmonic Group to play my *First Concerto in E-flat*. I trust I was not presuming on your time."

"Maestro, you know by now that *music* is my *time*, and if you think I am qualified for the piano part I will try to live up to your expectations. I am available for your extra students. Send them to my address."

CHAPTER 18

- 1886 -

Lest the reader become satiated with the mundane activities of the musician's world, I will skip over the next year and a half and come to 1886. Rose is now forty-two, looking thirty and Isobel reaching fourteen... with her poise and charm seeming twenty, were continuing to learn and develop what it took to realize their dreams.

This was to be a sad time for many. Father wrote: "Barnabus was buried next to Champion, his old stallion friend. Cat has left -- places unknown. Even the weather has been unsympathetic. The Queen was to open the International Exhibition of Navigation and Commerce in Liverpool, so she did, despite the worst rain storm for many years. The Royal Party just garbed themselves in waterproofs and parasols and drove on in an open landau. And now, your latest grief over your mentor and friend, Franz Liszt. You were fortunate, though, to have had a man of his greatness as an associate for so long. We are thinking of you and Isobel constantly. We long for you to hasten your coming to us. Father."

Yes, thought Rose, I have parted with many I have loved, but they've all left such sweet memories... I can only thank God that I've known them.

The area had been purchased for the Maria

Home and an architect selected -- who was none other than William Tilly, at Rose's request. In a month William would have completed his Berlin assignment and come to Bayreuth with Kathryn. The four would take a house near the construction site -- though it was not the most fashionable place by any means, it was large enough to accommodate Rose's studio, William's architect office, and privacy for everyone. There was a huge kitchen to the delight of Kathryn, who had become a fine culinary artist... and an herbal garden in the back of the house.

Bischofsgrun

The contractor working with William calculated the building would be completed and ready for use in late 1887. Isobel's school work was going very well, Rose had fifteen talented students, and Kathryn ran the house with one maid. Everything seemed too good to be true.

On the weekends the four would take a picnic lunch to the beautiful Red Main River -- and map out their coming trips to Fichtelgebirge -- a range of plateaus and granite mountains with thousands of conifers. A more ambitious trip was planned to go to Bischofsgrun where the longest ski lift in Europe was.

Rose was establishing a date in her mind that by 1890 matters would be settled and Maria House opened up. She would return to London and Isobel would be living in the 'House' as a trainee until her schooling was completed. Liszt's generosity had taken care of any unexpected financial need that might arise.

William Tilly had proved himself to be a fine designer and the contractor persuaded him to remain on in Bayreuth... the building business was booming... and Kathryn was quite pleased. Sooner than they had hoped Maria Ho. was opening its doors. The landscaping came next -- simple to begin with, but donations were coming in fast. Families no longer needing playground equipment: see-saws, sliding boards, swings and such, were dropping them off as donations.

In mid-1887 two little girls, one seven and the other eight years old, came to the 'Home' for admittance. 'Maria' undertook finding their origins and was told by a neighbor of the youngest child's parents that she was constantly beaten by a drunken father. After a visit to the welfare department of Bayreuth, she was told that they were overcrowded and could not take her, but they would investigate the girl's background, and... would gladly turn over several others if the 'Home' could accommodate them.

So a dream was coming true -- Maria House was dedicated and opened for homeless girls. The Mayor of Bayreuth conducted the ceremonies, gave the eulogies and cut the ribbon on the front door.

Things progressed as they should. Adjustments had to be made. The lady that had come to direct it temporarily was busy as a bee; new dresses were needed for the old rags they had worn on their little backs. The very next week a brand new baby girl was left on the front stoop in a basket. The card tied to the handle said: "Please take my poor baby... I have no money and I am not well." The little girls were crazy about the infant and took turns caring for her when they came in from school, which was only two blocks away.

Isobel asked Rose if it wouldn't be a good thing for her to go over and stay at Maria Ho. and be 'learning the ropes'? "I don't want to part with you yet, Isobel. Wait until September; besides we will leave soon for London."

England 1889

By June they were on their way. Carnelia was going to have her fifty-sixth birthday... and Rose was going to make it unforgettable. Father would take her to London for two days while the rest of the household got things at Hampstead in readiness for the surprise of her life. On Friday when the carriage drove up, Father and Carnelia walked down the path into the front foyer about four-thirty in the afternoon. Carnelia said she was dying for a cup of very hot tea. Cook said she'd serve her in the drawing room, and as she flung her shoes off... barely missing the chandelier... and slumped into the over-stuffed chair a shout went off: "Surprise! Surprise!" There seemed to be bodies jumping up from behind ferns, back of chairs, screens, sofas, everywhere. They all started singing a song that Sir Arthur Sullivan had just composed for the occasion, George du Maurier pulled in a wagon full of brightly colored packages that she must open while he sang to her. There was more rollicking good fun than she had ever experienced. Among the gifts were the song that Arthur had written, a love poem John had composed, a piece of needle-point that the Reverend Aston's wife had done, an ink-washing by du Maurier, a cake from a neighbor -- and on and on. Finally tea was set up on the lawn and all followed the honoree out.

Isobel's English was so improved since her last visit that one would take her for a native of England. She told the group that two more little girls were com-ing to Maria Ho. and that would make five children they'd saved from the street. "We have hired a house-keeper and a cook to help the directress," she added.

The remainder of the summer was spent riding horseback, playing croquet and tennis... and making lots of music. Arthur Sullivan asked Rose again when she was coming back to the Royal Academy and she told him her plans to accept the invitation to head up the piano department in 1889... about a year away. "I am leaving the children's project at Bayreuth in good hands. It will be partly supported by contributions and trust funds; as the children get older they will grow their own vegetables and learn to preserve them for winter use. They will make their own clothing and keep their rooms clean. When they have reached eighteen we will expect them to make their way in the world. We have very rigid rules about attending school and good decorum."

"I see you have been thorough about how an institution should be run. It was a wonderful party, and I apologize for staying so long... you must be very tired," and Sullivan left. His groomsmen had been killing time at Spaniard's Inn, but were waiting for him at the gate.

A beautifully illustrated book, *The Defense of Guinevere And Other Poems*, was hand-delivered to Rose the next day. They were from Sir Arthur Sullivan. She had merely mentioned that she was unfamiliar with the works of William Morris.

Later in the month they would go to Tintagel, on the northern coast of Cornwall. It would be a long trip, but trains were moving faster these days. Mr. Edleigh suggested making a two-day run of it by stopping for the night in Bath, a little more than half way to the coast. "I will look at the schedule and see if we can get an early start from Euston Station thereby reaching Bath before dark. I think Isobel will enjoy the old town.

Isobel was getting to be such a fine equestrian they decided she should enter the horse show. Gerald du Maurier was home from Harrow and went with Rose and Isobel to the tracks. To their great surprise, Isobel came in second place, and Snitzel got a huge horseshoe bouquet to go around her neck, which she immediately began eating on -- especially nice were the snapdragons!

Too bad that just when there was someone near her age close by, they would be leaving. A little summer would remain after they returned, though. Cook had packed a huge basket of picnic goodies and plenty of apple cider for the trip. How beautiful the rhododendrons were along the villages they passed.

"England is so wonderful and romantic, I hate to go back to Germany... but then that's my destiny... and it's what I must do. Yes, what I *want* to do! Rose, do you remember that frightened little urchin rooting in the ash cans?" and she reached over and threw her arms around Rose.

John Edleigh began telling them about Bath -- that it was founded, according to legend, by the father of King Lear whose name was Bladud, a prince who was banished from court as a leper. Bladud began to imitate the leprous swine of the forest by rolling in the warm mud where mineral waters had stagnated. But more likely it was the Romans who were first discoverers in about 44 B.C. They established elaborate steam baths, that even now are the most important relics left by the Roman conquerors in Britain. They called it Aqua Sulis. Then along came the Saxons, won over the city and called it Aet Bathum. In the middle ages it was a great cloth center. Later, about the 18th century, it was very fashionable as a watering-place. You will find that most of the buildings are in a yellowish-tan stone called Bath Stone. The chief things to see here are the Abbey Church, Roman baths, and the strange Pulteney Bridge. And when Isobel saw the bridge she exclaimed, "Oh, look, they've put funny houses on it."

"That can't compare with the curious Old London Bridge of 1600. The first settlement of London was probably started after the invasion of Claudius, a Roman Emperor. A crude river bridge of wood existed there on the Southwark side from the earliest Roman period. Then we know there was another bridge crossing the Thames in 1017 which was rebuilt in stone about 1200. And, of course, Old London Bridge was caught on fire in 1666. But soon as we get back home we are going to spend a day at the London Museum and see all the relics that have been found in the excavations.

"We should retire early, as we have an eight o'clock train in the morning in order to arrive in the late afternoon at Launceston. We can either spend the night there, or would you rather hire a carriage to go the rest of the way to Tintagel?"

"Let's do that," Rose suggested, "or wait and see how much daylight we have left when we leave the train."

So that was the plan agreed on. John Edleigh regretted they had so little time for Launceston; there was quite a bit to see, but they'd have to be content with the ancient round Norman castle that they glimpsed perched on the tall mound. "George Fox, the Quaker leader, was imprisoned in it for eight months in 1656 for passing out tracts that smacked of 'subversive literature.' It didn't seem to hurt him too severely: he married the widow of Judge Fell and inherited Swarthmoor Hall."

"'Scuse me, but what is a Quaker -- is it a Protestant?" asked Isobel.

"Yes, I guess it is a Protestant sect. They are known these days as 'Society of Friends.' There is a large building near Euston Station in London that is of that group. I understand there is a college in Pennsylvania, U.S.A., that was endowed by the Swarthmoors of Launceston. And there is a church here that someday we will get back to see. It has an intriguing history," said John. "We will need at least three days at Tintagel to get around to only a few of the many things of interest. Now, do you see why travel is so important to learning history and literature and, yes, art too. They stick in our memory when we've seen the places where they happened."

The night was comfortably spent at The King's Arms where Mr. Edleigh asked for a carriage and driver to hire for three days. Management said they would be at his disposal immediately after their breakfast.

"Wow! I've never had such fun," said the spirited Isobel, "and by the way, do I call you 'Father' or 'Mr. John'?"

"How's 'Daddy John' -- I would like that," said he.

"Do I really belong to you forever?"

"Of course, more so than if you were my natural child." ... At which remark Rose didn't take umbrage to -- she felt the same way about Isobel.

Leaving Launceston they skirted across the northern tip of Bodmin Moor, which all thought a dreary place. "One night when we are by the fireside back in Hampstead I'll tell you some pretty hair-raising tales about the Bodmin Moors. I'm glad it's daytime and not dark along this stretch."

In another hour they had gone through Davidstow -- just lots of pretty woods -- the rhododendrons were at their best. Then the driver told them they'd be making a little dog-leg from there on, as there was no direct road to Tintagel. He recommended King Arthur's Hotel. In another hour or so they would be at Tintagel with lots of the day left to explore. After registering and eating lunch they set out to look for King Arthur's Castle. Rose wasn't sure Isobel knew who Arthur was and asked if she knew anything about the opera based on the 'Round Table' where the knights of King Arthur sat... in a circle so as not to show any preference of one over another. "*Tristan and Isolde* is one of my favorites, by Wagner, and is very similar."

"Of course, everybody loves that one," Isobel replied.

"Well, our Arthur of Britanny was the son of Uther Pendragon and Ygrayne. It seems that the little baby Arthur was washed ashore near the magician Merlin's cave and he nurtured the child and taught him in Kingly ways. This was about the sixth century A.D. Arthur falls in love with Guinevere, but there is a love triangle with Lancelot, Arthur's trusted Knight. I'll tell you the story later. That's the way it was with Tristan and Isolde and King Mark. Right now we are going to climb this narrow path up the steep slate cliff to a promontory connected with the mainland by a rocky neck. Here, partly on the island and partly on the mainland, are the ruins of the castle. Don't look down unless you're holding on to the rail. The waters of the Bristol Channel almost converge with St. George's Channel and the crashing against the cliffs could break a ship into pieces." White foam was frothing and churning below where they stood. "But from the summit you can see the wild rugged shore from Trevose Head to Hartland Point."

They had had enough for a while and climbed back down the steep railed path. In the village they bought postcards to mail from the 'world's most beautiful post office,' a quaint old house of the thirteen hundreds. If their feet could have endured they would have liked to follow the shore eastward to Boscastle, but it was three and a half miles. They'd have to be driven there. It was a small village flanked by picturesque cliffs. The name was once Boltreaux Castle, but usage cut it to its present name. From there they could walk the one mile distance to Pentargon Bay with its beautiful waterfall and have tea. Close by was the setting of Thomas Hardy's *A Pair of Blue Eyes*. He got his inspiration while working as an architect on a church in the vicinity in 1872. A year later he wrote the novel.

The driver was helpful in pointing out many curious oddities that would have been overlooked. For tomorrow he suggested a drive to Clovelly. At the market, Rose bought a loaf of bread, cheese, ham, tomatoes and a sweet roll and prepared a basket. The hotel provided a little portable stove, so there was plenty of hot tea. The road to Clovelly would follow the north coast of Cornwall -- the first item of interest would be

Thomas Hardy

Penfound Manor that claims to be the oldest inhabited manor in England. It is part Saxon and Norman, with 16th century additions. The *Domesday Book* mentions it. Then we had to explain to Isobel that this book was a record of the survey of England made in 1086 by the Royal Agents of William the Conqueror. It listed the tenure, tenants and under-tenants with information about the values of properties, number of serfs and freemen. Today it's used for tracing genealogies and establishing boundary lines.

We all found Bude rather blah. So on to Kilkhampton where there's a large church of St. James's. It has a Norman south doorway and the organ was from Westminister Abbey, dating from about 1775. We returned to our main road, passing the woods of Stowe where the house of Richard Greenville was -- he had played an important role during the Civil Wars on the King's side against Cromwell, then passed through Stratton, a very pretty village. Returning to Bude we headed straight for Clovelly, a herring-fishing district, delightfully and uniquely situated in a narrow rift in the cliffs. It is so beautifully located that it is in danger of being over-populated with artists. The main street is far too steep for vehicles, so it descends in steps down 200 feet to a little cove and pier at the bottom. No two houses, with their green doors and boxes of cascading geraniums, are on the same level. The woods are so dense about the village that in winter its climate is extraordinarily mild.

The group decided to spread their blanket and unpack the basket for the noon meal. In the afternoon they took a sailing boat to the Isle of Lundy. That would fill the rest of the day. For tomorrow Isobel had requested Bodmin Moor -- if it wasn't too far. Tom

Hawks, the driver, said they could stay the night at Camelford... or maybe reach St. Breward... get an early start in the morning and have all day to prowl the moors reaching Bodmin by nightfall. The next day they could spend exploring the forbidding low hills to Bolventor.

The Knights of the Umbrella

Camelford came into view about dusk, and the driver being familiar with the next ten miles of travel on the lonely, desolate road, covered with fog, advised them to stay at the nearby inn. The quartet gladly left the creaking, swaying coach. Already the scenery had changed, promising the leanness and sparseness of a fiendish highway ahead.

But they slept well with a breeze blowing and rattling the windows so hard that they had to pull up the blankets round their necks. Next morning things looked more cheerful -- steaming hot tea does that for you. Off they ventured to the awesome moors. John Edleigh had heard about a notorious tavern at Bolventor whose owner was engaged in unlawful deeds. "It seems he took orders from a fiend that masked himself as a 'man of the cloth,' with a church not far away. Their business was one of misguiding trading ships into a false harbor where they would crash into the rocks. Then this tavern keeper with his cohorts would attack them by clubbing and drowning the ship's crew and stealing the cargo. This had been going on for a hundred years or more... passed down from family to fami-

ly." Isobel's eyes grew bigger and bigger. His tale fore-
told a day of excitement.

Jamaica Inn

"But what we are coming here to see is something
quite different," interrupted Tom Hawks. "Close to this
Jamacia Inn -- a house of bad repute -- is a body of
water that's called Dozmary Pool. To make it brief,
King Arthur was betrayed by Modred, who was accused
by Sir Bedivere of bringing the heathen back among the
King's house. And Arthur replied to Bedivere 'yet one
last act of Knighthood shalt thou see ere I pass.' Utter-
ing this the King struck out at Modred, but Modred
smote his liege so hard that Arthur had barely enough
strength to strike back, but with that one blow killed

Modred with his sword Excalibur.

"Then the King said to Bedivere, 'take my brand Excalibur, which was my pride, and return it from whence it came. But now delay not; take Excalibur and fling him in the middle of the mere, watch what thou seest, and bring me word.'

"So Bedivere went to the lake, but was so bewitched by the beauty of the sword with its topaz lights, twinkling diamond sparks and jacinth work of subtle gems -- he could not hurl it into the water. So he concealed it in the foliage along the lake's edge, and strode slowly back to the King.

"'Didst thou perform my mission? What did you see... and what did you hear?' And Bedivere, not able to reply rightly, was sent again. He attempted the second time to cast Excalibur into the lake -- but then he saw the wonder of the hilt -- how marvelously chased... and cried out that surely so precious a thing should not be lost from the world. He failed again, reasoning how nice 'twould be to store it in a treasure house saying to future generations: 'King Arthur's Sword, Excalibur, wrought by the lonely maiden of the Lake. Nine years she was in fashioning it.' So he hid it a second time and returned at a sluggish pace to the King.

"Then King Arthur, nearing his end, asked again, 'What sawest thou and heardst?' Sir Bedivere lied, saying, 'I heard the water lapping on the crag, and the long ripple washing in the reeds.'

"Now Arthur was angry. 'Ah, miserable and unkind, untrue, unknightly, traitor-hearted! Woe is me! Thou wouldst betray me for the precious hilt -- or like a girl valuing the giddy pleasure of the eyes. Get thou hence: but if thou spare to fling Excalibur this third time, I will arise and slay thee with my hands!'

"And you can bet that this time Sir Bedivere leaped down to the edges of the water -- through the bulrushes, clutched the hidden sword and wheeled it round and threw it into the lake. The sword made lightnings in the splendor of the moon and before touching the water it shot like a streamer and flashed blindingly toward the surface, but just before hitting the water an arm arose, clothed in a heavy silk fabric shot through with silver and gold threads, and caught Excalibur and drew him under the mere!

"And then Bedivere went back to the King with quickened steps. 'Now I see the deed is done by the look of your eye. What didst thou see and hear?' said the King.

"Bedivere replied that he had to close his eyes lest he should have been blinded by the gleam of the gems, but when I flung him in, an arm clothed in samite caught him by the hilt, brandished him three times and drew him 'neath the water.

"The king breathing hard said his end drew nigh, 'Carry me to the lake.'

"There they saw a dusky barge and Arthur murmured, 'Place me inside by the crowned Queens.'

"When Sir Bedivere cried out, 'Ah, my Lord Arthur, whether shall I go? -- I see the old times are dead -- the whole Round Table is dissolved. And now I go alone among new men, strange faces, other minds.'

"And Arthur with his last breath spake from the barge, 'The old order changeth, yielding place to new. God fulfill Himself in many ways -- if thou shouldst not see my face again, pray for my soul. More things are wrought by prayer than this world dreams of... For what are men better than sheeps or goats that nourish a blind life within a brain, if, knowing God, they lift not

hands of prayer for both themselves and those who call
them friend?'

"The barge with oar and sail moved from the
brink. Sir Bedivere stood long... looking at the disap-
pearing vessel until it was one black dot upon the horizon."

Rose, Mr. Edleigh, Carnelia and Isobel were
amazed at the articulation of their driver. And Rose
thought of another young guide she'd known in Berlin
that was working for his architectural degree. Life kept
repeating itself in situations. She hoped Isobel was too
young for his Thespian talents to work their magic on
her.

"Well," said Mr. Edleigh, "I never got that much
out of Tennyson when I went to Oxford as you have
given us. But how small the lake looks!" They all got

out of the carriage to get a better view. "But what a large imagination the Poet had," said Tom Hawks, "I did my treatise on Alfred, Lord Tennyson. I hate to spoil the romance, but I don't believe the lake is more than six feet deep at any spot in it. Now let's return to the carriage."

The Culprit Emerges

They were very hungry. "My, but this is a lonely stretch of road; we haven't seen a sign of man or beast since we left Camelford," sighed Carnelia.

"It isn't likely that you will either, until the Bodmin coach comes along early tomorrow morning. That is why we waited until after nine today to leave; it has arrived at Launceston by now. So, ladies and gentleman, you have been very nice company to be with, but if you will kindly hand me your purses and jewelry we will part best of acquaintances,"
-- and he gave his gun a twirl. John Edleigh placed his wallet, watch and jeweled tie pin into Hawks' outstretched hat and Carnelia leaned over her husband fumbling with her rings, purse and other trinkets. Rose spied her father's umbrella on the floor, nudged Isobel -- who caught her signal -- and with Hawks' back turned away from them... Isobel slipped the curved handle around

the bandit's ankle. Both girls, pulling on the other
end, brought Hawks down to the floor of the narrow
aisle. While he flipped, John reached for the flying
pistol.
It was a desperate move, but they were in desperate
straits!

Mr. Edleigh turned to the fellow and said, "Out,
Mr. Tom Hawks, you can await the next diligence to
Launceston -- and I believe you said *tomorrow morning*.
Your vehicle will be at the railway station, for we do
not steal from people!"

Hunger was forgotten -- at least by John, Rose,
Carnelia and Isobel as they flew down the road to the
nearest town, which was Trewint, and to the constable's
office. There would be a mighty hungry guy struggling
down the road to Jamaica Inn. Constable Helmes immediately retraced their journey -- about ten miles -- to
the vicinity of Dozmary Pool. There they found the
culprit hiding at the deserted Jamaica Inn. Hawks was
handcuffed and brought back to Trewint for identifica-
tion.

"Just as I suspected," said Helmes, "the young
fellow who pulled the same stunt up on Exmoor, in
Somerset near the Devon Line -- hasn't changed his
style. He applies at Inns as a guide-driver for tourists
who want to see the Lorna Doone country, especially
where the Doone gang were supposed to hang out --
bandits, they were too. This fellow Hawks was quite an
actor... Blackmore, the author, couldn't have told the
legend better."

"But not good enough for the Actor's Guild -- I
wasn't able to get a job performing on stage... but maybe on a *stagecoach*. I got in bad money deals and in
trouble with a barkeeper's daughter in Minehead: I

needed funds in a hurry to get her out of town. Her father would have killed us both," said Tom Hawks.

"Yep, the prisons are full of dramatic cases. I don't believe it necessary to keep you good people here any longer. Be on your way with better luck," said the lawman. An authorized driver took the Edleighs on to Launceston where they caught a night coach back to peaceful Hampstead Heath. It had all happened so quickly they hadn't a chance to bask in its brilliance... its bravado.

CHAPTER 19

Bayreuth

Next week was parting time for the Edleigh family. Rose and Isobel back to Bayreuth, Germany. "Father, we will not come home for Christmas... I feel we ought to spend it at 'Maria House' with the children. It would be merry if you and Carnelia visited us, there's so much room."

Isobel enrolled in the College for Women in Bayreuth. It was a small institution, but well-accredited. She lived in the Maria Ho., located within walking distance.

Upon returning to Germany, they found that two new girls had come to them, making seven children ranging in age from six months to thirteen years old. The piano was in continuous use what with Rose's fifteen students and her own practicing. By December first she would present them in recital in the College for Women's auditorium.

And the time flew -- the trees turned red and orange and finally blew away leaving the limbs and branches shivering in the sudden light snow. Then in late November everything was pure white, with silvery icicles hanging around... and Rose was reminded of the samite-clothed arm that drew Excalibur under the mere. Oh, my! Bless the old umbrella with the over-sized handle that had tripped up their poet-laureate bandit --

how she could use it now against this falling blanket of snow! She fell to daydreaming, picturing the four of them dragging along the lonely road, hungry and thirsty and with not a pence in their purse. Well, as their desperado had quoted King Arthur: "More things are wrought by prayer than this world dreams of"... if an old umbrella handle could work miracles -- how much *more* humans should be tools from whom great wonders could be wrought!

After the November recital Rose was approached by the Dean of the Academy, but Rose declined, thanking him for the offer. She told him that in June she would return to her native England; she was only in Germany until the Maria House was running properly.

Upon reaching her quarters she found a letter from Father stating that he was giving a piano to the Maria Ho., he would wait until he got to Bayreuth in mid-December to purchase it -- as freight cost was exorbitant. Everyone sent love and he just couldn't wait for their reunion. They would put on a Christmas that the little ones at the home had never known the likes of.

"All Hampstead Heath calls the Edleighs 'heroes of the moors' after that hold-up at Bolventor. Love, Father."

The Eve of the great day finally came. No Christmas had ever been more festive than this one. The piano for Maria Ho. arrived two days before. The generosity of the people of Bayreuth was overwhelming; they had sent warm, almost new, coats for the girls; needlework and yarn for their finger's activity; toys and food -- everything. But the part they were looking forward to most was going caroling. They made quite a procession... the nine children, the four Edleighs, Kathryn, William and the Directress padding out in the powdery snow singing their hearts out with joy. People all along the street opened their doors and asked them in for chocolate, steaming hot.

When they finally got to bed, Mr. Edleigh came into the parlour with a basket under his arms. "Oh-h!" Carnelia had already guessed what it contained! Yes, a small St. Bernard puppy. "Every house needs a dog about the place," exclaimed John. But that wasn't his real reason. He just couldn't resist the little four-legger at the pet shop.

"Whose stocking are you putting that in?" asked Carnelia -- as if she hadn't already guessed it was for Isobel.

The blessed holiday was over and things returned to normal. Isobel loved being in college... and coming home at night to the children at "Maria's."

May 1890... Farewell to Germany

Rose's time had come to leave Bayreuth. Many wonderful things had happened here -- sad things, too. She went once more to Wagner's and Liszt's graves and put a bouquet on each. Then Isobel and she visited Isobel's mother's plot.

Next week they would be back in England. There were now ten little girls at "Maria's" that would be missing Isobel. Barnabus the 3rd came out to say good-bye in his puppy way. The children had taught him to shake hands. He was the image of the other two 'Barns' in Rose's life. Isobel would be back with them in September -- but not Rose, so she picked up each child

Isobel

and hugged her. She told them that there would be a
young teacher in to give piano lessons to those who
desired to learn to play. "Please come back for our
next Christmas," the children all chorused, as she was
driven away.

John Edleigh was retiring from his position at the
Royal Exchange; he was approaching his sixty-sixth
birthday -- almost forty years of which he had been with
the same firm. He was given a spectacular send-off;
and after emptying his desk left for Hampstead Heath
to enjoy being lazy. He was in for a rude shock when
he discovered he couldn't break his old habit of rising
very early and shaving hurriedly to catch the train in for
London. So he decided to take up horseback riding
each day before breakfast.

Rose went back to her old faculty dormitory at
the Royal Academy of Music where she headed the
Piano Department. Her schedule was rather heavy,
making it impossible for her to return to Hampstead
except on the weekends. The Edleighs frequently came
to town and had lunch or dinner at her convenience.

In October Rose was invited to tea at the
Claridge Hotel with Sir Arthur Sullivan. There was so
much to talk about... tea had to be re-warmed many
times before they took out time to sip. Sullivan asked
Rose if she knew much about Gustav Mahler. "Only
slightly," said she.

"I heard his *First Symphony* in Budapest recently
when I was over on the Continent for holiday and attended a concert where it was being played. I found his
music very interesting; he is one of the first, for a long
time, to use contrapuntal style. We find some in Beethoven. Yes, I rather liked Mahler. He had a sorta'
hard time in Vienna... making very little headway to-

ward glory there. Opportunities were plentiful in many opera houses, but he had a way of grating on people's nerves... on the stage and in the pit. His compositions demanded so much of the orchestras and the singers that they turned from him. It was mutual. He hated the opera because of the insufficiencies around him and the time it took from his composing. His *Songs of a Wayfarer* was quite beautiful, but unsung. The *First Symphony* was written while he was here, but the small audience found it unromantic; 'it wailed, it screamed in anguish, was ablast with hell, itself!' 1888 had been a bad year all around for Mahler -- but he started on his *Second Symphony* before he left."

There'd been so much tragedy the past year..... Emperor Franz Josef with his constant avarice toward his son, the Crown Prince Rudolf, that went on and on until it climaxed in tragic results. Rudolf had been restless. He was put-down firmly by his over-bearing father. The Empress Elizabeth, in her memoirs, noted that there was such a change in the Prince: he was distraught and given to outbursts of temper.

Rudolf became involved in secret journalism. He confided to Moritz Szeps, harping on the fact that war must come soon -- "otherwise we can never build a great and wonderful Austria." He *meant* war with Russia! Through it he thought to gain glory for himself. The war with Russia didn't happen... but a young woman named Mary Vetsera did! All else was falling apart in Rudolf's life -- he needed something fresh and inspiring and found it in the company of the sweet and gentle Vetsera girl... and she reciprocated. She wrote her governess that "if I could give my life to make him happy I would gladly do it." This went on in secrecy. Rudolf forgot all his disappointments in the fulfillment of their little liaisons.

Vienna was in a morbid slump. Suicides seemed to be daily occurrences. Then suddenly in December every thing went into a spin the other way. The city became like a masqued ball -- entertainment and self indulgence became paramount. Rudolf was becoming more and more involved with Mary Vetsera. It has always been noted that depressed persons become more acutely so during merry seasons. The Prince was tottering on the brink of despair; the thought of suicide was constantly with him. He confided it to Mary -- and she cried and embraced him; she would happily become his partner in a death pact. He craved the feeling of 'no longer being alive.' Together they arranged the date and the procedure. They would go to his hunting lodge at Mayerling and there carry out the plans. That was January 28, 1889.

Fifteen miles from the carnival city of Vienna Rudolf and Mary went to their last trysting place. The Prince told his loyal servant to call him at 7:30 sharp the next morning.

All the gongs in China could not awaken the two. The door was locked and bolted. An axe finally opened up a hole in the entry -- and the tool immediately dropped. The dull thud of silence from the room was to change an Empire.

"But let's hear from you, Rose. How did you leave things in Bayreuth?"

She told Sullivan about the Maria Ho. "They now have ten children, a nice piano, a music teacher -- a St. Bernard dog -- and you know how *that* got there! My dreams are really working out. Isobel has two more years of college, then she will take over the directorate."

"Did the Emperor ever realize what you did with

the necklace he presented to you?"

"Yes, and he sent gifts to the institution. We don't call it that, though. It's always 'Maria.'"

Christmas seemed to come faster and faster as Rose grew older. Days flew by with her teaching and her public concerts. In fact she was to play at Buckingham Palace in late November. When she was at her father's on the past weekend, they discussed going to Bayreuth to see that the children's Christmas was merry!

"Oh, ho," said Rose, "they've gotten to you, haven't they?"

There was an overflowing audience at Buckingham Palace. Rose played a Frescobaldi number first, followed by a Brahms "Rhapsody," "Un Sospiro" of Chopin, "Fantasia Impromptu," and ending with her own "By Crystal Waters."

The London Times wrote: "The artist stands at the full height of virtuosity. Her playing was with effortless skill and good taste. A pianist to be proclaimed as a leading musician of her times."

The three Edleighs left in mid-December for Bayreuth. They were beginning to feel like half-German and half-English with all the trapesing back and forth. The nineteenth century was soon coming to an end -- no century had known such changes in human thought and feelings: Darwin's theories of struggle for existence; survival of the fittest, natural selection, denial of inheritance, and acquired characteristics... all going to make up his *Origin of Species* had its effect on some, but all of it swirled in an orb of nothingness over Rose's head. She believed, as Nanny taught her, in the infallibility of the Scriptures. The Victorian Era was slipping away -- losing its influence on literature. Dickens and Balzac were being labeled "romantic dribble" -- passé. Now the trend was toward the naturalistic novel, expressed by its leader, Emile Zola, following the theories of Darwin. Though Charles Darwin died in 1882, he had planted many dangerous seed that would bear fruit in the next generation.

All was serene in Rose's life... God was in His heaven -- everything was right in *her* world. The Maria Ho. had its beautiful Christmas season. Mr. Edleigh rented a Santa Claus outfit and practiced his 'ho, ho, ho's.' Some of the children that remembered last year's party asked Rose why her father didn't come this time. She answered that he'd be there later. "Well, it's too bad he'll be missing Santa," said an eight-year-old.

All good things have to come to an end -- not that
going back to England wasn't good! But they hated
leaving the little ones.

The Dying of an Innocent Century

In the preceding year, General William B. Booth
published his "In Darkest England"; he initiated a charity fund to rescue the 'submerged tenth of the population' who were steeped in vice and poverty. The Queen
wished him great success in his undertaking. In two
months the fund had grown to 80,000 pounds -- but this
was not a tenth of the amount needed, according to the
General's estimate. This movement became the founding of the Salvation Army, which spread world-wide.
Already by 1890 the results were starting to show.

The next few years went by in a rhythmical pat-
tern... except their trips to Bayreuth were fewer; Isobel
did the traveling back and forth instead. The Maria
Ho. had been in operation for ten years now and there
were fifty girls that had been taken in, ranging from one
year to seventeen years in age.

Rose became a 'fixture' at the Royal Academy of

Music in London. She would be forty-seven on her next birthday. Recently she had concertized in Munich, Vienna and Rome. The schedule fitted in with a little excursion to Bavaria to see Neuschwanstein Castle. King Ludwig II had been dead since June, 1886. Carnelia was aghast at such a monstrosity of a building.

"I think it's romantic," marveled Rose. "There has been so much tragedy: two royal personages -- third-cousins dying only three years apart -- both murders and suicides. Most people believe Ludwig arranged his own death by drowning. It was hard to understand how a good swimmer should be able to commit suicide in such shallow water; so some said it was a heart attack. But Ernest Newman concluded the murder explanation was the correct one. The King knew that life was over for him when he was confined to Berg Schloss on the Starnberg lake side. The Empress Elizabeth was visiting her mother at Possenhofen, only across the lake from the tragedy, when she heard the news. She cried out, "The King was *not* mad -- only an 'eccentric' living in his own dream world!"

"You do remember our visit to the von Miller's home, years ago, don't you? Well, from their lake pier you could have seen the cross that now marks the spot where poor Ludwig was found. Anyway the world is richer for his having been here, as Wagner owed so much of his success to his patronage. Not only that, but the country that hated his spending all that money on his 'follies' is now getting it back from the tourists that visit his palaces. And wasn't it strange that Elizabeth, Franz Josef's Empress, died so tragically a dozen or more years later by an assassin's stab," said Rose.

"Well, I'm glad we're just plain folks," was John's comment.

Vienna's concert went off successfully, as it had in Munich, followed by the third in Rome. In Rome they remained on a few days longer to visit the great monuments. Rose wanted to see the Appian Way where St. Paul trod his last steps to his martyrdom. They passed the Pyramid of Cestius, near St. Paul's Gate -- and the 'Three Taverns.' Rose had felt her emotions surfacing as they walked along the same old worn stones, laid in 312 B.C. by Appius Claudius Caecus --, just as St. Paul had done. Rose took out her New Testament and turned to 'The Acts'. In Chapter 28 it described exactly the spot where they were as the road that Paul entered after the terrible ship wreck. He, then, was being taken to Rome to be tried by Caesar. The ship had battled a wretched storm and its crew was without food and water for 14 days. They finally arrived at Rhegium -- and the next day at Puteoli -- then the Appius Forum. Puteoli was near Naples, about 100 miles south of Rome.

Rose asked Father if it were too late to visit the Roman Forum and enter the Mamertine Prison where Paul wrote his last letters to Timothy. "No, we'll take a cab; I'd like to go there very much... and you, Carnelia?" So they were off -- Father reminding them both to clutch their bags tightly, and avoid contact with people.

The driver put them out at the entrance close to the Portico of the Dili Consentes, an elegant colonnade honoring the twelve deities -- next came the Temple of Vespasian and from there they entered the Mamertine Prison. Rose remarked on its smallness and the stone seat that ran along the side of the walls. "Just think... about eighteen hundred and twenty-four years ago a man sat here writing letters of comfort to his friends...

and today we can pick up a Bible and read those same words. That, in itself, is a miracle. I've never had this feeling before, not so vividly."

The Vatican — Rome

CHAPTER 20

Hampstead Heath -- 1892

Getting home again was always like a renewal of life. The first news they received was that George du Maurier's novel *Trilby* was a huge success. One might say that it was this book alone that made him a rich man. It was read avidly, both in England and America. Then *Peter Ibbetson* followed it; the reading public found it delightful.

But nothing had changed George... he was still the fellow they'd all known and whose sweet voice made everyone forget his troubles. "I shall never forget that *'voix d'or'*!" said John.

Isobel wrote frequently from Bayreuth news of the different children's accomplishments. "We now have seventy-five girls, and are having to have an additional dormitory built -- and of course William and Kathryn come over very often. Kathryn is taking over a few of the better students in piano. We are preparing to stage a musical production of *Romeo and Juliet* -- and I think it's good! We may invite the Lord Mayor of Bayreuth to attend."

This brought a great deal of satisfaction to Rose: to think that God had allowed her to play this part in making the world a little nicer place.

In England, Queen Victoria was having her troubles -- with nine children, almost every one married to a

225

foreign Prince, Grand Duke, or Emperor -- with all their deaths and war troubles brewing; this was enough for an 'ordinary' mother! But the Queen had a realm to rule and she took it seriously. Her relationship with her ministers was the most important segment in her well-being. In 1893, one burden was lifted: Gladstone retired. When particularly angered by his liberal policies she often referred to him as her 'thorn in the flesh -- that man *Galdstone*'! When Disraeli retired she was faced with the possibility of having Gladstone as her Prime Minister; she had made it abundantly plain that after his conduct in the Russo-Turkish War she was determined never to allow him to hold office again. When told by Granville and Hartington that he was the only one who could command a majority in the Commons -- the Queen said that she would abdicate in such consequences. In the end she gave in. She and Gladstone clashed on foreign affairs: hers was a vision of great Empires. Gladstone looked on such aggressiveness as morally wrong. What finally drove him into retirement was his quarrel over Ireland. Personally, Queen Victoria could never understand 'those Irish' and really didn't much care for them. After Peel's death there was no one to speak for the Irish, as he was the only one sympathetic to their problems. Much disorder, crime and murder was being committed there, and she blamed Gladstone not only for not quelling it, but rather pandering to it.

The next few years found Victoria softening toward the Irish. The Boers and Uitlanders (foreigners) came to war, and things got bad for Britain. But some comfort came from the fact that the colonies sent forces to help the Motherland. It wasn't until she visited the hospital in a wheelchair that she came into contact with

Irish soldiers -- she was touched by their valor, and by the end of 1900 had made her first visit ever to Ireland.

The Queen struggled on until the end of 1900. But on New Year's Day, 1901, she was wasted and tired. Her zest for her duties had left her. In January, on the 22nd, surrounded by her family, Victoria drew her last breath. It devastated the people of Britain. She was put to rest next to her beloved Albert in the sarcophagus at Frogmore, Windsor Castle.

The year 1900 had been a sad one for the Royal House, but not half so much as for Rose: he had been her best friend and mentor -- England's greatest musician; Sir Arthur Sullivan's death was felt all over the country. He was only two years older than Rose, but had contributed so much during his brief life. He would always be remembered for *The Mikado*, *Pinafore*, and his fine church music. Another bright star had fallen from the skies of the "Innocent Century," but the glow of his musical art would never lose its luster.

Edward VII

Now a new reign would start. King Edward VII, at long last, would occupy the throne... long over due. To the Englishman at this time the French were still a subject of a mixture of mild ridicule and downright apprehension. In this mutual disharmony -- France felt about the same way toward England -- it was unlikely there would be much affection.

But for a short time it seemed like a leaning toward Germany was taking place... perhaps only superficially. The Kaiser had played the part of a devoted grandson to Queen Victoria, but never quite lived up to the role of respectful nephew to Prince Edward. After Edward VII had inherited the throne, the Kaiser tried to warm up to the King, but fortunately British policy directors who had once looked upon Germany as a possible ally, began to change their view to one of a probable rival.

In Edward's love of travel he took a Mediterranean cruise, including a visit to the Pope, returning home overland by way of Paris. There he made a speech that silenced that old jargon: 'the English don't like us'; they had been screaming *Vivent les Boers,*" "*Vive Fashoda,*" reminding him of old hatreds.

But after Edward's speech which had touched on the pleasure of being in Paris, and complimented France "as champions and pioneers of peaceful progress and civilization"... he remarked on their culture that produced the noblest in art, science and literature... then there was a turn-about in relationship between the two countries. As he drove away he was wildly cheered. This was Edward's first move toward diplomatic achievement. The Anglo-French Conventions of 1904 had settled most of their old controversies.

Back in England, two years later, changes were taking place. There was staged a general election; the Liberals made their moves. In the same year, just before New Year there was a demonstration in the Albert Hall: ladies were clamoring for the right to vote.

- 1906 -

In Hampstead Heath nothing of this touched the Edleighs -- except the loss of the beloved Queen and the success of the new King Edward. They were not 'shirkers' -- but they did believe in, and lived by the old song "Brighten the Corner Where You Are." Charity and humility described this strongly-knit family... and many a stray piece of humanity found its way to their door with outstretched hand and left filled to the brim.

Berlin and London pretended international cour-

tesy and decency, but this was a facade. The whole
world looked on -- they saw with suspicion the possible
production of a 13.5 inch naval gun... and the new
Zepplin performing in the air, also the machine-gun
department at the army maneuvers.

Lord Asquith was fidgety about it all -- the future
looked bad. Edward VII was back in London now
making his customary rounds. One evening was spent
hearing the concert at the Royal Academy, where he
heard an English lady play. He noted the name Rose
Edleigh on his program. Her playing took his mind off
the political and military situation for a while. A musician for England to be proud of, he thought.

Edward's health, never sturdy, was failing. "I shall
work to the end. Of what use is it to be alive if one
cannot work?" But on the morning of May 7, 1910, the
reign of King George V began with the death of his
father, Edward VII.

- 1911 -

At the Academy, Rose was invited to make a tour
to the United States the next year in 1912. This was to
top all her past concertizing. The desire on her part
was to accept -- but then she worried about the type of
audience she would be playing for. They, the Americans, were a new breed. Did they like the fiery technical works of a Godowsky-Chopin *A Flat Etude*, which is
exasperatingly difficult; the *Don Juan Fantasie* of Liszt -
- or would they lean to the Debussys or Ravels? The
giants of the keyboard: Brahms, de Pachmann and

Liszt always seem to be reaching out for an orchestral expression... sounds beyond the limitations of the piano-forte. She discussed it with her peers at the Academy and they all agreed: give them one number to show off your ability of execution... then choose the rest from what you like to play.

So she signed the contract. Her program would consist of the *Brahms-Paganini Variations* and the Beethoven, *Opus 106* for ear-openers. From there she would select Debussy's *Homage 'a Rameau*, and *Jardins sous la Pluie*. The last group would be her own compositions: "Sad Song" and "The Voices of the Sea." On the final number, even in the 8,000 capacity auditorium, the very softest, sweetest tones must be heard in the last row of the rear seats. She must capture the listener and make her instrument supreme in every soul in the hall.

The year 1911 was passing with Rose harder at work and more disciplined in life-style than she'd ever been before. The Edleighs would accompany her to America. John Edleigh had a startling idea, "Why don't we try to get a booking on the new steamship *Titanic*. It would sail from Southampton April 10 on her maiden voyage. That will give us eight months to make our plans; but first I must inquire about accommodations available for three persons."

Carnelia and Rose thought the adventure would be wonderful. So early next morning John got started. He called the British White Star Line; they had only three openings resulting from cancellations the day before.

That was all they could talk about for the next few days; their excitement was so fervent that the news headlines screaming from the London papers about the second war scare in Morocco didn't put a dent in their

ardor for this new venture. The ship was *unsinkable...*
852 feet long with a 92.6 foot beam, tonnage 46,308 and
speed 21 knots.

But the rest of Britain was in alarm. The French
made public their plan to occupy several Moroccan
towns because, they said, the lives of Europeans were
not safe. For breaking the Algeciras agreement Germany determined to make France pay an indemnity.
When she was ignored she sent the gunboat *Panther* to
settle it in the Agadir harbor. British were frightened
because the presence of a warship meant that Germany
would place a naval base in Morocco on the Atlantic
coast. The Moroccan question was temporarily settled,
though, giving France a free hand in Morocco, but
awarding a hundred thousand square-mile tract in the
French Congo to Germany. Deep down, most of the
people thought a serious conflict was bound to happen
sooner or later.

Late August, 1911

One Sunday afternoon a mood of nostalgic memories began flooding Rose's thoughts... the old times --
the horses they had loved and lost -- Nanny, yes, Nanny
and her wonderful gingerbread. Father was out in the
garden with his pipe, pretending to be useful with the
pruning shears, and Carnelia was working a piece of pe-
tit point to use on the seedy-looking sofa pillow that
had been around since Barnabus I had yanked at it and
dragged it all over the house.

From the top shelf of the bookcase Rose got
down the recipes that Nanny had used. There she

found the one for raisin ginger squares. She checked the larder and found all the ingredients. It was Cook's day off -- or she would be fuming over the mess Rose was making with the flour and spices. Soon she had them in the oven... and now would clean up the pre-baking catastrophe before any of the family came in to see what she was doing. In about thirty minutes vapors started filling the kitchen, wafting their way down the pantry hall, into the drawing room, and out the sun room windows. John Edleigh straightened his back and took a few whiffs and reaching for his spectacles followed the pungent fragrance to its source. "Oh ho, time for tea, yes?" said he.

"I hope they taste like Nanny's used to... I just got homesick for the way things once were," said Rose.

"What's the matter with the way things are now," chided her father. Then in came Carnelia sniffing her way to the delicious area. The three sat at the kitchen table, all manners dropped, and dove into the hot bread which had been spread with clotted cream.

"Why, Rose, I didn't know you could bake! We'll have the du Mauriers and a few others over for an old-fashioned tea. Is next Sunday all right?"

Rose could not get over the fact that 'little Gerald', who had taught Isobel to play tennis, was now a matinee idol to the London theatre crowd. They had seen several of his plays at Wyndham's Theatre. He had made his first formal appearance as *Raffles*, a play brimming with action from beginning to end. He enthralled the audience. In 1910 Gerald had gone into theatre management, having acted in many of Sir James Barrie's plays: *The Admirable Crichton* (1902); *Peter Pan* (1904); *Alice-Sit-by-the-Fire* (1905); *What Every Woman Knows* (1908); and more. And to think he now had three young daughters Jeanne, Angela and Daphne. (Daphne would some day excel the genius of her father and grandfather.)

Social functions in Hampstead had never been the same since George du Maurier died in 1896. But they were fortunate to have the son Gerald to come to tea when he had no matinee performance. They would always bring the three girls. They would certainly liven things up... especially Daphne. And, of course, the prospects of Rose's gingerbread would entice them any time.

And fall came... the leaves twirled down from the boughs and covered the ground with a yellow, red and brown carpet. As December approached they thought about the children at Bayreuth... but this year they would have to miss their usual holiday with them. Isobel was so swamped in her duties at the Maria House that, could they have secured passage for her, she would not have been able to make the trip to America.

CHAPTER 21

1912... Tragedy at Sea

The American voyage was two days away. Mr. Edleigh announced he would go into London to see his lawyer; he'd let things slide for so long that now he must put his estate matters in order. It was a quite simple transaction. Mainly, Carnelia would live in their home or dispose of it as she saw fit... but sharing equally with Rose... Hampstead House and all the buildings connected with it plus household furnishings and livestock.

Now his mind was settled and he could look forward to the coming venture. The train would take them to Southampton, where the *Titanic* would begin her maiden voyage the next day, April 10th. The atmosphere was heavy from all the excitement. The three walked up the boarding ramp to the main deck of the ship. What a wonder! Each side of the deck was filled with little shops and lovely sidewalk cafes. Flowers were everywhere. A stewart helped them to their suite, as complete as a fine hotel. There they unpacked and settled in for a bit, then went out to the promenade deck. One hour passed, then two... and still all the sights were unseen yet. Several ships had been spotted as they passed. John said there were twenty-two hundred persons aboard. Their course would take them toward Newfoundland. The ship's progress could be charted on a wall map designed for that purpose.

The four days aboard were like a grand fantastic dream. Many notable persons were on the passenger list... some the Edleighs recognized from their often-photographed faces in the London papers. It was like a big fashionable spa. On the second night out the recreational director had a party; the dining area was made to look like a beach with umbrellas attached to each table and the waitresses dressed in two-piece bathing suits. Carnelia pointed out John Jacob Astor to Rose, "He's the one whose uncle, William Waldorf Astor, was the grandson of the first John J. Astor who made a great fortune in fur trading. The old man was a German, but moved to America and *his* son was William Bachouse Astor, called 'the Landlord of New York', and the son that followed was William Waldorf Astor, U. S. Minister to Italy. At the end of the 19th century he went to England and bought Hever Castle to display his wealth. He also owned several newspapers and tried his hand at writing... mediocre fiction, they said. Well, this one sitting at your right is his nephew."

"Well, I'm completely at sea about all your lineage, but he's the nephew of the 'Hever Astors'... is that right?" asked Rose.

"Yes, he's John J. Astor IV."

Tomorrow would be their fifth day out -- and Rose wished it would go on forever like this. But fate had something different in mind.

"I'm tuckered out," said John Edleigh... "celebrities or not, I'm going to bed." And all followed. It was only 11:00 p.m., but there had been so much noise; when the band wasn't playing, the wireless was blasting with silly announcements about different passengers aboard.

All of a sudden there was a blunt thud, throwing

several pieces off the night stand. How fast they seemed to have been going! It was 11:40. Plants and tables began to topple over; what on earth was happening! The Edleighs got dressed and went to the deckway.

For some time passing ships had tried to warn *Titanic* of a pending disaster, but the Marconi Stations were so busy with their own trifling news and entertainment program that they heard no warnings coming from the *Friedrech Wilhelm* of the North German Lloyd Line -- they were unable to break through *Titanic's* programming. As soon as Commander E. J. Smith realized something was amiss it was too late. At a speed of more than 21 knots *Titanic* had hit an iceberg. Now all passengers were on deck. Women were slipping on life-preservers, with ship's personnel helping to adjust them. They had started lining up on deck A, port side. The three Edleighs clung together. Passengers on deck saw the *California*, which sailors assumed to be four miles away, and it kept their courage up -- until the beacons became dim and blackened out. It was still uppermost in everyone's mind that *Titanic* was unsinkable... and there was no real danger.

Down in the radio room little attention was paid to messages sent from passing ships: the *California* of the Leyland Line had wired the *Titanic* saying they were stuck in surrounding broken-up icebergs. The too-bibulous operators of the wireless replied, "Shut up, we're busy."

Then came the blast of Commander Smith's voice from the bullhorn to the crewmen to lower the lifeboats... "Women and children first." Father turned to them, "Go, you heard the order!" But Carnelia and Rose wouldn't budge. "I'll not take a step without Carnelia," replied Rose, to which Carnelia responded, "I'll not leave John's side. Now get going, *you* have a concert tour contract to honor."

"As if that's a reason for being separated from you two!"

"You leave us now or we'll both jump overboard right this minute!" commanded the parents.

Rose was a child again... "Yes, Father, see you both at Carnegie Hall," and she climbed into the lifeboat as if she were a mechanical doll, powered by a wind-up thing-a-ma-jig. She felt the k-plunk when the craft hit the water... then she must have blacked out for

a long period of time. When consciousness returned she looked about her at the benumbed faces of her fellow passengers. A jug of water was passed among them with hunks of bread. Nobody seemed to know how long they had rowed about in the icy waters, but at last a ship bearing the name *Carpathian* was pulling them in to safety. It was April 15, 4:10 a.m. The sailors managing the rescue told the boat survivors that *Titanic* went down about 2:20 a.m., and according to the wireless many hundreds of persons were carried with her.

Somewhere in New York harbor the *Carpathian* docked. The group that was pulled from the water was taken to a nearby hospital for quarantine and observation. Rose had lost all track of time. She held on to a strong belief that her parents had been saved somehow.

It was Monday morning, April 18th. She had been given some hospital gowns and robes to wear while her clothes dried out. Fortunately, she had clung to her purse and had information inside about her appointments and her passport. Everything came back in focus now. She was to meet the director of the "New York Music Lover's Series" at the Waldorf-Astoria Hotel on April 25th at noon. And with the revival of her memory she realized she had not touched a piano in a week -- and what would she wear! And where were her parents! Everyday she gleamed through all the newspapers to read about lifeboats being picked up at all coastal areas along the Eastern U. S. waterfronts. Each day a few drowned bodies would be washed ashore. Findings were scattered for many miles -- sometimes over an area of 65 miles apart. Improvised morgues were set up to try to identify the dead; the unclaimed list stood at more than sixty.

Rose decided the best thing to do was to cable her father's lawyer in London. He was unable to be in his office because of illness, but his partner was available and much acquainted with what was going on. Mr. Sakew cabled back that he would arrive by the next sailing and would come to the Waldorf-Astoria to her.

The hotel just could not do enough for Rose; they considered her the greatest heroine they had ever hosted. A Fifth Avenue Boutique contributed an evening gown for her concert with all the accessories to match.

It was now April 22 and Rose had a place to practice at the hotel. She had stipulated in the contract that the two center seats on the first row were not to be sold, they were for her parents. So strong was her faith, that she still thought they might be occupied... that somehow they would show up at the last moment....

The day came. Rose was rested and anticipating her concert. She dressed with care. At 7:20 she was picked up by a limousine for Carnegie Hall. There was a half-hour before starting time and she sat alone in her dressing room with the door closed... and in the silence she remembered every detail of the last moments on the ill-fated *Titanic*. Her words, "See you at Carnegie Hall" faded into a reply almost snuffed out by the howling wind... "Save us two seats, front row!"

Then a knock on the door. The call-boy told her it was time to start. And she shook off her memories and strode out to the center of the stage. The noise from clapping hands in the auditorium was thunderous -- like the sound of a stampeding herd of bulls -- but suddenly came to a deadening silence. The entire audience arose in respect for the brave survivor of the tragedy that was now felt by the whole world. Rose bowed deep in acceptance of this expression of sympathy. She was moved to respond, "This concert is given in honor of my beloved parents, whose spirits must occupy the two empty seats before me."

The nine-foot Steinway beckoned her with its gleaming white ivories awaiting the Brahms-Paganini "Variations." Her performance was characterized by splendid technique, excellent phrasing and a caressing touch; the less critical ear only heard the pleasing sound that filled the Hall. The Beethoven followed; it had vitality and gusto about it which lent an air of authority

and importance to the pianist. Now they could relax --
here was someone who deserved the price of their tick-
et. They loved the Debussy numbers. Her last piece
seemed to have been chosen, prophetically, months
beforehand... "Voices From the Sea," one of her own
compositions. When her finger sounded that last sigh
and she lifted it from the keys -- there were no 'bravos',
no clapping. Only a dead stillness. She walked to the
edge of the stage and bowed low. As she straightened
to face the audience they all stood mutely until she
turned to leave the stage. Then the crowd became a
tumultuous outburst of passion and admiration. She
was gone. In her dressing room she dried her eyes and
went with the chauffeur to the hotel.

Rose found her room at the Waldorf filled with
flowers -- the cards bore names she'd never heard of.
She collapsed on the bed and fell asleep in all her formal finery. It was after midnight when she awoke and
changed to her night clothes. This was the 26th of
April; on the second of May she was to play in Boston.
She certainly hoped to feel more rested by then. She
was so very tired -- after all she'd been through, no
wonder, she thought. Tomorrow a little practicing and
reading and she'd have room service bring her meals.
The concierge found a map of Massachusetts and she
read up on the city of Boston. The enlarged inset
showed Symphony Hall at Huntington and Massachusetts Avenues.

When her lunch was brought in, there was the
New York Times and a note from the desk telling her to
see page eighteen. Thumbing through the pages she
came to the review of her performance of the night before. It really would have gone to her head if she were-
n't such an unpretentious, modest person. It read:

"Saved from the Atlantic tragedy to bring pleasure and joy to New York concert-goers." The write-up filled a quarter of the page -- and affected her so strangely. She fell to her knees and thanked her Creator for the gift of music. "And, Precious Lord, use my life as You desire. Help those in pain, hunger, and sadness. And those Thou hast chosen, keep them safely in Thy bosom until called to a greater glory with Thee. Amen. -- And, Father, why am I so tired? Help me to honor my commitments."

Rose got up from her knees. There was a knock at the door. She opened it to Jason Sakew and a lady who accompanied him. After introductions he explained that knowing the ordeals she had suffered, the Law Firm thought she needed a companion-nurse. Miss Addie Mason was highly recommended.

"Oh, Mr. Sakew, I didn't realize prayers were answered so quickly. Please sit down, I was just going to order tea."

"I am leaving the day after tomorrow. I will see the Morgan Guaranty and Trust Bank about a fund that you can draw from; you are very well fixed along financial lines. Do you remember the property of your deceased grandfather in Alabama... Selma, I believe it was? That is also in your name and at your disposal."

"Yes, I remember going there once with Father and Carnelia -- a beautiful little town with much colourful history. How long ago that was! I was in my late twenties, about forty years ago.

"Tonight you will dine with Miss Mason and me at the hotel. They will bring in another bed so that she can stay in the room with me," said Rose.

"Oh, yes, I am staying at the Waldorf until I leave. Then you and Miss Addie can travel on to Boston."

The next morning Rose felt exhausted, dispirited. Miss Addie said, "My dear, you need to get out in the fresh sunshine, it's lovely today."

Rose hesitated -- "But I don't think I feel like dressing... I have a terrible aching in my arms and shoulders."

Miss Addie assured her she was coming down with a cold. "But I can hardly move my upper back," said Rose as the thermometer was pushed in her mouth. It read 102°.

"I am going to call a doctor, the concierge says there is a good one in an office next to the hotel."

The physician diagnosed a bad cold and left a prescription for Addie to have filled.

When Mr. Sakew came the next day to say good-bye, he looked a bit concerned. The fever was still there and Rose had a difficult time sitting up in bed. She reached to shake hands with the lawyer and to thank him, but her right shoulder wouldn't respond.

He asked Miss Addie to come with him for a cup of tea -- and she hastily got her bag and said to Rose, "I'll be back in a moment." Out of Rose's hearing, Mr. Sakew said, "I don't like the way she looks. I'm not satisfied with that doctor's verdict. I want to call in a specialist for a second opinion. Meanwhile we must wire Boston and cancel her concert. They will certainly understand the situation."

The new doctor came promptly, even though it was his afternoon off. He laid aside his golf bags and picked up his medical bag instead. He looked at Rose and took her temperature... 103°. He turned to Mr. Sakew and said, "It doesn't look good -- I have had over a hundred cases of infantile paralysis this year. The epidemic of 1911 was the worst this city has ever known, and it hasn't abated yet. With all the trauma this lady has had lately she would be a good candidate for this terrible disease." After many pokes and jabs at Rose's painful areas, he pronounced quarantine in the hospital.

Mr. Sakew left for England, but Miss Addie remained on with Rose. He would cable back as soon as he reached London. Boston understood about the cancellation and its necessity and assured them they could get a replacement... maybe not as crowd-attracting, however. Rose was subjected to hot baths three and four times a day and the therapy was lounging in the sun room while Addie read to her.

After a month the doctor thought she should find a quieter place than the Waldorf... and besides it must be costing her a fortune there. Addie got busy looking; the hotel concierge was a great help; he knew just the place. So Addie went to the address, took a good going over of the neighborhood, saw there was a Nauheim chemist on the corner that also served short food orders. The flat was on the street level not far from one of the main entrances to Central Park. The doctor's prognosis was good -- until he learned from Addie that Rose was a concert pianist. Then he dropped his eyes and sadly shook his head; at her age he did not believe she would be able to regain the required dexterity in the right hand. "In fact, I offer no hope along those lines."

It was a horrible blow to Rose, but she didn't go into a dramatic scene over it.

"Addie, we can see all the wonderful sights New York has to offer -- and when we've exhausted those, we'll get my property down in the South fixed up and go there."

"Where is 'there,' dear?"

"Oh, didn't I tell you about Alabama? My ancestors were there before the Revolution. They had lived in Devonshire, England, and there was a lot of unrest in that region. I have heard that a Thomas Poderfoy lost his right arm at White Plains, New York.

"Addie, isn't White Plains close by here? And didn't I lose my right arm here, too? This is ironic. Get me a book on "The American Revolution" at the book store when you go out."

Addie was delighted to see Rose come to life... they would read together.   That afternoon Addie pushed Rose's chair across Riverside Drive where the pigeons made much to-do over her anticipated arrival with her sack of crumbs. The wheelchair seemed to be so clumsy for her companion to maneuver; Rose suggested they hire the doorman's son to handle it for her. He was a nice fellow in his middle teens and could use the spare money.

Sam, that was his name, accepted the offer excitedly and started his services the next day. He suggested they go down Riverside Drive as far as Grant's Tomb, explaining to the English ladies who Grant was. Sam proved to be quite a source of knowledge... a wonderful guide. Over the tomb was carved Grant's words: "Let us have peace." It reminded Rose of Napoleon's tomb in the Invalides at Paris. The interior contained twin sarcophagi with the remains of General and Mrs. Grant in the crypt. The Civil War had ended almost 50 years before, but the memorial was only 15 years old.

July in New York was extremely hot. Sam told Rose about "Jones Beach" and the cool Atlantic breeze... then suddenly became mute. He thought he had been callous to mention the Atlantic, knowing that it was a bad memory to Miss Edleigh. He blushed and begged her pardon. "It's all right, Sam, please don't feel bad." And to prove it, she exclaimed enthusiastically, "Do you suppose there's any way for us to get there and take a picnic basket?"

Sam answered that he'd ask his father about it -- the wheelchair might present a problem. "But there is a place we can go tomorrow, if you'd like: 'Cleopatra's Needle'; there are two others in the world like this one here, one on the Thames Embankment -- and I've forgotten where the other is. They were quarried by Thothmes III (Thutmose) in 1500 B.C. We studied about Thothmes in history last year. That's my favorite subject. Thothmes built a huge fleet and conquered the islands all the way to the Aegean Sea. Someday I'm going to see all the treasures of the world."

"That's a very fine goal, Sam. Get your college behind you first; a knowledge of languages is very important if you are going to really enjoy travel in foreign countries."

And the summer passed, fall appeared and Rose was sixty-nine years old... though she said nothing on her birthday to anyone. She was gaining strength and felt more reliable on her feet, but the right shoulder still needed frequent, very hot bathings. It was frustrating to not have any feelings in her arm or fingers... and especially not being able to move them.

Miss Addie cautioned Sam behind Rose's back not to mention the concerts in Central Park in the evenings... or anything to do with music. "Yes, Mam, but why?"

"Oh, Miss Edleigh was the most brilliant woman pianist since Olga Samaroff; she gave her last concert at Carnegie Hall a week or so after the *Titanic* sank last April."

"I felt like there was something special about her. May I tell my father? He is a great music lover."

"No, don't tell a soul -- that's *our* secret. I will let you read her news reviews if you promise to seal your lips."

"Yes, Mam," said Sam. "You know, last year I lost my best friend from infantile paralysis. They had to close the schools here to help stop the spread."

The trio -- two ladies and a boy pushing a wheel-chair, became a fixture in the neighborhood. They had visited all the museums and art galleries in Upper West Section. The days were growing shorter and Sam was back in school, so they saw very little of him these days. The pigeons seemed to be leaving the parkway on Riverside Drive. Miss Addie could see a listlessness coming over Rose. So little to do. "I'm going to get a typewriter for you and you're going to start writing your autobiography."

"I'm too old to start typing... even if I had *two* hands," she protested.

"Too old, my tail feathers! -- you're just sinking into a slough -- and I'm not going to stand for that! You can fire me if you like, but I've come to loving you too much to see you vegetate and nurse your self-pity."

Neither spoke for a long time... then Rose admitted Addie was right. "Get the thing -- I'll 'hunt and peck' with my left hand 'til I've conquered it."

"That's my girl. You shall have it tomorrow." And Addie consulted Mr. Anderson, the doorman, who knew where to shop for just about anything. While she was out, Rose got daring and thought she might make it to the bench on the corner of West End Avenue and 82nd Street, a little over a block away. She did, and felt like she had 'crossed her Rubicon'. Sitting there, breathing hard, and eyes closed momentarily, a strange feeling came over her. On opening her lids there was a huge dog staring at her -- a St. Bernard with the most soulful eyes. He laid his head on her lap -- and Rose cried, "Oh, Barnabus, where did you come from... you wonderful beast!"

A few moments later the dog's master appeared; a cultivated gentleman in his seventies, Rose thought.

"So, my Henrietta has found a friend. May I sit beside you and rest my weary bones?"

"Please do, I am Rose Edleigh. I had a dog like that once... in fact three of them: Barnabus I, Barnabus II, and Barnabus III. They are all at rest now in England."

"Yes, I was going to ask if you were not from the London area. I could tell from your accent; I once taught courses in Psychology in London, but am now retired and live close by."

"So do I. In fact I see my companion coming this way. Addie, this is Mr. -- er -- what was the name again?"

"I'm so sorry, I forgot to introduce myself -- absent minded professor, you know. It's Townsend... James is what my friends call me. How do you do, Miss Addie?"

"Rose! What on earth are you doing here all alone? How did you get here... where's your wheelchair?"

"I used this cane -- and I'm free. Addie, I'm free again! Professor Townsend taught Psychology in London..."

"Well, you could take some advice from him, my lady, about big cities like New York. Have you never heard of the gang wars and hoodlums," Addie interrupted, "I'm amazed at your naive judgement, Rose."

Rose laughed, "I guess the Lord takes care of old fools and little children."

"And drunks... none of which you are," retorted Addie, too furious to acknowledge the introduction of Mr. James Townsend... (only the most sought after lecturer in the metropolis!).

"Ladies, have a good afternoon. May I walk you home? My Henrietta will be a detriment to any harm-doer."

It was time now for Addie's apologies to the new-comer -- and she went to extremes and invited the professor to accompany them and stop in for tea.

"But, my dog."

"Oh, he'll be fine. Mr. Anderson loves animals and allows them inside. So let's be moving along," as she helped Rose to her feet and handed her the cane. The four trudged at Rose's pace for the short distance to their apartment.

Addie soon realized that Rose's new friend was indeed a gentleman. He and Rose discovered they had a mutual friend: both knew Gerald du Maurier very well. Professor Townsend praised his Thespian brilliance in the 1906 portrayal of "Raffles", an action-packed production from start to finish. Rose had also seen it and agreed. She told her guest about Gerald's childhood and his having grown up in Hampstead Heath... attending many soireés at their home with his father, George."

"And the *Ware Case* in which Hubert Ware murdered his brother-in-law, drowning him in a lake and lying all the way to the trial, aided by a good-for-nothing accomplice. Gerald came to me in my last year at the University and asked my opinion on the immoral influence it would have on the audience. I couldn't answer him -- so it remained ponderously on his conscience. I don't know if the play was ever done or not."

Addie brought in a biscuit for Henrietta, which she refused, to the embarrassment of her master. The guest pulled out his watch and said, "Dear ladies, do you know that Henrietta gets her bad manners from me... I have long overstayed my visit, and am afraid I have inconvenienced my hostesses. Shall we have tea at my place next week... Thursday? My man will pick you up at four in the afternoon."

With their assenting nod he walked toward the door and turned to them, "Until then, my friends," and he and Henrietta departed.

The next day was Thanksgiving Day -- so Rose and Addie were introduced to their first 'turkey feast.' They almost sympathized with their colonial ancestors when they learned that there were two sides to the conflict between the Brits and the Colonists. "I don't believe my tea is quite the same any more -- to think of the blood shed over a little spot of tea leaf liquid!"

"It wasn't the tea's fault, it was the taxation on it," said Addie.

When the appointed day came, Mr. Townsend sent his chauffeur to Rose's address and with the driver and doorman's help she managed getting seated in the car.

"What a lovely home you have, Professor; do you live alone?"

"Yes, since my wife died many years ago. I am thinking of making a trip back to England in May -- mostly to retrace some of our happy days together there," and pointing to the portrait over the fireplace he explained that she was only twenty-five when it was painted, and not long afterwards she died. I've never talked about her to anyone else around here... I don't know why I've opened up to you about her."

"Well, I have some cherished secrets that I don't share, but I feel like telling you. I was a concert pianist; studied under Liszt and Sullivan and was teaching at the Royal Academy of Music when I received a request to tour America..." Rose could get no further. She turned her head, and Addie went to her side, "Now, now, dearest. That's enough for today. May we have our wraps, Mr. Townsend. It's been a lovely afternoon -- and shall we host you next Thursday?"

It was agreed on. How peculiar it was when Addie and James Townsend found themselves buying the "Times" at the same vendor's stand two days later. "Oh, Mr. Townsend, my Rose has scarcely said a word since we last saw you. Things have started tumbling in on her. I can't make it out... her depression. I do hope you can cheer her up when you come Thursday."

"I will do my best, Miss Addie. Good to meet you on this beautiful day."

On Thursday, Rose said to her companion, "Just look at this dinnerware; not exactly Wedgwood, eh! I hate to serve tea to Mr. Townsend in this dismal pottery. We'll just have to make up for it with your tasty pastry."

"Some flowers will do lots for this old table top. So I'll run down to the vendor's stall and select something -- I 'spose all they will have will be poinsettias, it being so close to Christmas," and Addie threw on her coat and swept out the door.

At four o'clock Mr. Townsend rang their bell. There was Henrietta by his side all excited and nudging his way in ahead of everyone. His gulping down of the tarts and ginger snaps was very complimentary to

Addie. And while she was clearing up the mess, Rose found a chance to talk confidentially with the psychologist, "I am very depressed -- the inactivity and worthlessness of my life have me down. I am thinking of moving south for a while and trying it out."

"My dear, I think there's sense in that idea. You've given up returning to England, then? What about the adopted sister in Bayreuth, could she come and visit with you?"

"I had a letter from her only this morning. My father's lawyer had communicated with her and gave her my address. She wants to come see me here in New York."

"Perhaps that will cheer you."

"Yes, but then she has her own life with the Maria House... it would be for only a few days. She says that the house in Hampstead is closed up and the servants all retired except for the gardener who still tends the grounds and airs the house weekly. The lawyer has had our passports extended."

Mr. Townsend announced that he'd be delighted to have the company of the ladies at a little party he was giving in two weeks... and might he have them picked up by Jarvis on the 22nd of December. Addie answered that they'd be happy to accept.

These little get-togethers continued until the approaching spring months at which time Rose anticipated Isobel's visit... also saddened, though, by the departure of her friend who would be in England for six months. Mr. Townsend talked professionally to Rose advising her to settle in a small community where the weather was more moderate, and do a little gardening. So Rose was sure now that she would have the Alabama house put in shape and give it a try.

Spring arrived and Isobel with it. How they clung to one another at the ship dock! "Well, if you two ever get unclenched the taxi driver will be waiting -- and no doubt the meter has been running for fifteen minutes already," called the thrifty Addie, with her fingers drumming on her purse.

When they were settled, Isobel collapsed on the sofa, exhausted from the long trip from Bayreuth... "Oh Rose, some of our older 'children' have really done well since they got out into the world. We're very proud of all of them. We've only had one rebellious child; one who was impossible from the start. She wreaked havoc from the moment she arrive at the 'home' until she finally ran away for good -- at least for *our* good! I do still pray for her wherever she is... Poor thing, maybe 'life' will teach her!"

Isobel turned to Addie and said, "This Maria House is what Rose accomplished while studying music with Franz Liszt in Germany. She found me surviving on garbage dumps and loved me into a human being."

Addie told her to wait a minute while she fetched her German-English dictionary to enable her to communicate with the lady. Even Rose's German vocabulary was a bit rusty from nonuse, as Isobel's English was. But through a sign language and hard concentration they managed. Rose suggested a light supper and early retiring to be rested for the next day.

At breakfast Isobel assured Rose that William and Kathryn Tilly would write immediately when they learned her address. "So I have dropped them a letter telling them all about the things that have occurred to you since 1911. They will catch us up on the news in Germany. When I left there were some sentiments expressed that were very unsettling. Kaiser Wilhelm is getting restless and rattling his great collection of armaments. It seems the Kaiser is licking his chops to get at France for some reason. I don't understand all that's going on... they seem friendly enough with the United States; but to tell the truth I'm a little afraid. William will understand the matters better than I. So we'll forget all that and just be happy that we're together."

"Isobel, I have decided to move to Alabama; that's way south of here -- to a small town called Selma. I am not happy here in New York, as so much reminds me of my handicap: not being able to play piano again has been like ripping out my very heart. I can see the musical notes in my mind's eye... and sometimes I become so frustrated I want to run and run and never stop until I fall and know nothing ever again."

"Oh, Rose, please don't talk that way. Music is what brought you to my rescue... and I'm sure the Creator has a purpose in taking it away for a while."

"You're right, my dear. No more tears. Look out, Alabama, here I come!"

CHAPTER 22

1914 -- America

And *War* came! It was now 1914. Isobel had returned home several months ago to Bayreuth, but Rose had heard from William Tilly that at mid-morning on a shiny bright August day, 1914, about a half a dozen German cavalrymen dressed in their military regalia which consisted of ornate helmets and frightening sabers marched up to a French sentry post at a house close to the border town of Belfort. A challenge was yelled out by a French corporal named Peugeot. The German lieutenant halted, drew his pistol and fired. The first bullet dug into a tree, the second one into Peugeot's chest and the third into a plum tree which splintered into chips. Before dying Peugeot managed to hoist his rifle and send three shots into the German. The Frenchman staggered a bit and fell dead on the doorsteps of the house. The First World War had started.

In the last weeks of July the Austrian Archduke Franz Ferdinand was assassinated by a nineteen year old Slav at Sarajevo. Serbia was blamed for the attack, so an ultimatum was flashed across Europe. "I don't know what this is all going to come to, but, my dearest friend, it can't effect *our* mutual feelings. Kathryn is aghast! We are both neutral about war matters: we live in a world apart from politics. I suppose there'll be no more work for architects for a while -- I'm old enough to retire anyway. Kathryn and I live at Maria House now, in a cottage on the grounds. She still teaches piano and I'm something of a handy man. If war comes to *us* pray the children at the 'House' are safe.

"I don't know how much longer we can get mail overseas, but we'll keep you informed as much as possible about Isobel and the little ones. I believe you said your new address will be Selma, Alabama, Lamar Avenue. Please confirm that."

Rose put the letter down and explained things to Addie. Addie, who was hard to get 'worked-up' over future happenings said that she would go with Rose and get her settled down in the 'peat bogs and the wild Indians'.

"Oh, Addie, you don't know what you're talking about. I've been there before with Father -- many years ago. It's a beautiful little city. It was the arsenal of the South during the Civil War -- and don't you know we British aided the Confederates, as they were called, in that struggle. The Poderfoy house is not a large one -- in fact very unassuming in appearance, but there's space in the back for kitchen gardening. You'll like it."

The paper boys on the street were screaming headlines. Addie went to the window: "Austria-Hungary declares war on Serbia!"

"Quick, go buy a paper; I want to know what's going on." She read: "Russia mobilized to protect its ally, Serbia. Germany to aid its ally Austria by threatening to march against Russia and France. If Germany invaded Belgium, Britain vowed to fight her. It was spreading fast and was feared that Austria-Hungary, Serbia, France, Belgium, Britain, Russia and Germany were officially at war."

Both ladies' faces were drawn with worry... and Addie immediately ran to the kitchen for tea, which always seemed to make things a little saner.

"I have word that the house will be in shape for us to arrive there by mid-September. We must communicate with the consul to look into the status of our passports, if Mr. Sakew hasn't already done so. We're going to make it a jolly adventure in spite of the gloom and doom across the Channel," said Rose, perking up. "What did you put in that tea, Addie? Come now, up to your old tricks to liven the party!"

Every day there was news of new outbreaks in Europe. The massive right wing of the German Army swept into Belgium, swinging west toward the English Channel and down into the heart of France -- only thirty miles from Paris. Young men were conscripted by the Germans, French and British -- all chewed up by the grinding machine of war!

Rose could take no more and went to bed where she lay awake until the break of day. How could she pass the time 'til September. The typing was going well... she was disciplined from her piano practice of so many years. She'd developed her own system: A-B, A-B, -- A-C, A-C, -- A-D, etc., through the entire alphabet with her left fingers. Chapter One was finished on her *Memoirs*. Addie wanted her to read it to her -- and was astonished at her flair for story-telling. This encouraged Rose, so the time passed faster. She closed her tablet and put it aside.

With so little to pack, as she had done shopping for necessary wardrobe only, they were ready to leave. Addie was good about business transactions; she called the Pennsylvania Railroad Station for two one-way reservations to Selma, Alabama, on the 15th of September. They would be in a sleeper for two nights and their destination reached on the seventeenth. Rose communicated with her lawyer in London and he would arrange for her banking deposits to be received by a Selma bank. He assured her the house was in readiness for her, but she should spend the first night at the Albert Hotel, as that was where she could get the keys to the Poderfoy place.

The taxi driver had been summoned by Mr. Anderson, and his son, Sam, would ride with them to the station. Rose made Sam promise that if she stayed South for good that he would spend a summer with her. That tickled him to death: he could learn firsthand all the history of the Civil War.

When the train left the station, Addie and Rose sat back against the plush cut-velvet seat and drew a sigh of relief. The scenery was quite interesting: no thatched roofs or cobble-stone lanes or quaint villages... just woods, woods, and more woods for two days.

Upon finally pulling into the Selma Station, they took a cab to the Albert -- it seemed like only yesterday she made this same trek. Addie looked to her left and saw a sheer drop with a brown river running in its bottom making a path far below. Rose told her about the fame of that bluff. Once Lafayette landed there in the early eighteen-hundreds on his way to Cahaba, the capital of Alabama at that time. Selma was not unknown to many of the world's famous such as DeSoto, the Duke of Saxe-Weimar, Sarah Bernhardt (actress) and Enrico Caruso.

"Because of the high bluff, this was the best fortified city in the South. But we have time to talk about that later."

Their compartment was comfortable and clean; the service was really excellent. Both women slept wonderfully -- if Addie felt a bit squeamish about tomahawks and soft silent moccasins she said nothing at breakfast. They were then driven to Lamar Avenue, with the nervous Addie wondering what to expect. She was a little surprised to find an ordinary clapboard-framed house -- no fluted columns, no tall Tudor chimneys, no gazebos.

"Here we are," said Rose. "Not what you expected, is it, Addie? Well, it's home for the present time." Rose felt good about it... Addie went straight to the kitchen. The big wood stove, the oilcloth on the table, the cupboard and pantry were adequate. But best of all there was a neighborhood grocery store in the next block. In the back was a vacant lot and Addie called to Rose, "Come, look! There's a huge cemetery on the street behind this one; have you ever seen so many monuments and statues?"

But Rose was occupied at another window where she saw a fleeting figure of a little girl darting from tree to tree -- evidently spying on the two old ladies that were going to live in the house next door. Rose was stunned for a moment -- her head swam as though she were going to faint. Addie came running to her side. "Addie, it's Isobel! It's my Isobel!" A cold towel was placed on Rose's forehead. And she soon was herself again.

"Oh, dear, you're very tired. Let Addie make you something hot."

While sipping the tea a beautiful melody drifted into the room. Somewhere someone was playing a simple Clementi Sonatina. It was no amateur-sounding rendition. The trills and mordents were executed with

A little girl darting from tree to tree — spying

the skill of a promising artist. Then she looked toward the window but there was no little 'Sherlock' darting around obstacles. The music had stopped: an adult voice called, "Wendy, you're not practicing! Get back to the piano!"

The two houses were so close together that Rose had to laugh when she recalled the lawyers referring to the 'Poderfoy estate'.

A knock at the door summoned Addie... there stood a little knock-kneed girl with a fist full of daffodils. It was all too much for the frail Rose. Tears were welling up in her eyes. "Come in, child. Are you

Wendy? Were you playing the piano?"

"Oh yes, ma'am, I'm going to be a concert player...
if Mama doesn't kill me first," and she broke into laughter. "She gets very angry if I stop before my hour is up.
My name is Wendy Hoberson and you are Rose and the
other lady is Addie."

"And I think you are 'Mr. Watson' -- Mr. Holmes
is more formal than *you*! We are so happy to live next
door to you, Wendy," said Rose.

"Can I come over when I want to see you -- I get
so tired of kids -- kids -- kids. Some of them are pains
in the you-know-what!"

"Yes, indeed. Will you have tea with Miss Addie
and me tomorrow at four o'clock?"

"Mama won't let me drink tea -- I'll bring the
lemonade. Bye."

Tea the next day was a big success. Rose knew
everybody in town before thirty minutes was over. And
leaving the house Wendy warned: "and look out for
that 'old sweater man' that comes around."

"Who's *he*?"

"I don't know -- some of the older kids talk about
him, but I've never seen him, and don't wanta!"

"Come again, child. It was a wonderful visit -- and
when you practice, leave the window open so I can hear
you."

Selma was a peculiar town, it seemed to Addie:
the Negroes all stayed to themselves, the white people
were rather a conglomeration of souls, the Jews owned
all the stores and just as in England the 'old money'
didn't mix with the 'new money.' Rose and her companion enjoyed slow walks to the river bluff and some-
days went to the cemetery to sit in the shade of the old
'live-oak' trees. But the best times were when Wendy

and her friends would come over for gingerbread and stories.

Rose and Addie knew of the terrible death throes that were raging in Europe and they grieved about them, but at the same time thankful for the neutral stand the United States was taking. They prayed for the safety of William and Kathryn Tilly and Isobel in Bayreuth. They received no news from them, though.

CHAPTER 23

February 1915

The victory in the World War depended on the control of the seas. The British blockade was causing doom to Germany and unless she could break it in some way all was lost for Germany. President Wilson had warned them about the International law regarding merchantmen and informed the German government that they would be held accountable for any acts that jeopardized the lives or property of American citizens. But Germany ignored this and sent out submarines to sink England's *Lusitania* which had Americans on board.

Even after this breach, America was divided on the issue of getting into war. Then in March, 1916, a German sub attacked a French passenger ship that injured several Americans. Germany then sent out something in the way of an apology. This had a slightly calming effect, but not for long. President Wilson offered some principles upon which a lasting peace could come about, but stated that "only peace with a victory" would bring a permanent settlement. These efforts seemed worthless. So the Allied Governments knew that war must be fought to a conclusive result; on January 31, 1917, submarine warfare was resumed.

Wilson called a special session of the Sixty-fifth Congress -- and a state of war was announced against

Germany.

It was a shock to the people of this small city, but the volunteers came pouring in. Wendy's Uncle Luman was among the first to leave for duty. She spent more time with the ladies next door, and they explained all the reasons for the war. "And, Rose, you know that awful 'Kaiser Bill' was the grandson of our beloved Queen Victoria," said Addie.

Nationwide in the United States the draft bill received a world of criticism -- some of the smaller places felt more patriotism than the larger cities. Many agreed that there was a scant difference between 'convict' and 'conscript'. It took Congress six weeks after the declaration of war to get around to passing the Conscription Bill. Some doom-hawkers prophesied that there would be blood flowing in the streets of America over this civil disagreement.

All males between eighteen and forty-five had to register for "selective duty." That meant the draftee would be drafted for duty where he was most useful. Soon things settled and cooled off -- there were added some exemptions to war service for men in key industries. By registration day all the country seemed to accept the inevitable and there was much flag waving... there would be no blood running in the streets.

Women were admitted for the first time into the armed forces and were called "Yeomanettes" if they were Navy, and "Marinettes" if in the Marine Corps.

Everybody was singing "Johnny, get your gun, get your gun..." and "Over There". But 'over there' was making dramatic changes: Germany knocked Russia out of the war very early in 1918. This suddenly released hundreds of thousands of German veterans to the front in France. Berlin was counting on doing away with Great Britain in six months -- long before America would make up her mind to enter the conflict, they thought. Germany also underestimated the U.S. in being able to transport their army so far from home base. To their surprise, there was a sprawling 225 miles of American barracks and over a hundred hospitals in France.

In the spring of 1918, the terrible German drive exploded. There were half a million well-trained troops moving to the Western Front with deadly momentum. The Supreme Commander Marshal Foch finally united the Allies and coordinated their activities.

The Americans were coming, finally, but almost too late. Germany was smashing toward France intending to eliminate her from the war, when American troops, 30,000 of them, showed up at Château-Thierry where they were a blessing in helping to stem the tide. By June, Belleau Wood was cleared of the Germans. The French in gratitude renamed the place "Marine Woods."

Up to this time, the War of 1917 was our best-fought war.

Wendy finally felt all this talk was over her head. She just wanted her Uncle Luman back, and soon!

It was time for the morning mail, and Brooks, the postman, went to the door of Miss Rose's house and knocked. "Miss Edleigh, there seems to be an awfully important letter here for your friend... it has so many stamps on it, must be from England."

"Thank you, Brooks, it is for Miss Addie; her family lives in Sussex, England."

"Well, I hope it's good news," as he walked away.

Addie tore it open nervously. It was from a friend of her kin telling her that her brother was very ill, near death, and in his delirium was asking for her.

"Oh, Rose, Rose. What can I do!" Should I try to make it home. I feel I should. There will be family matters to settle and I'm about the only one left. But how can I leave you?"

"Certainly, you must go. I can get along fine; a yardman will help me with the heavy work. We will set about to find out what ships are sailing and when."... And the terrible panic that seized her at the thoughts of an ocean crossing had to be repressed; she must hide her apprehension of that devouring body of water.

Some passenger liners were in operation, in fact there was such an influx of foreigners flocking to the 'Promised Land of America,' that a restriction was being demanded that allowed only a hundred and fifty thousand immigrants a year -- so the ships would be returning to England practically empty. Rose's banker helped them with the details of Addie's maneuvers: train tickets to New York, ship schedule, and transportation from Southampton to Sussex.

"Oh, Rose, will I see you again?"

"Yes, love, when all this gets settled. You have been my angel of mercy; how could I have survived without you! I will just keep up my writing on the book -- and thank you for making me do it. It has helped me get so many things out in the open. I just pretend, now, that I'm some one else reading about a character named Rose."

"Perhaps you'll get back to Hampstead in the near future -- maybe before I can return to Selma," said Addie.

"No, Addie, I'll never go back. My life is here; I love this place. I will get along fine. After all, I've only lost the use of one hand. Think of all the soldiers returning from war with only a leg or 'two stumps' -- and worse: those that were gassed in action. And I have my dear little friends who come over for stories."

But that wasn't the real truth; Rose had lost everything that was dear to her of the past. Only the Maria House would be a reminder of her former years... If she could only hear from them over there in that defeated country of Germany.

Next week Addie would be leaving. Autumn was on them... never had the trees been so colorful. The maples were delirious, blushing in all shades of red and orange, and the late roses and yellow chrysanthemums were in full array. At least there would be 'no mourning when Addie put out to sea.'

Rose asked Wendy if she wanted to accompany them in the taxi to the train station. Mama gave her consent. Wendy brought out some divinity candy and fruit cake that her mother had baked for Addie's journey with a note of apology for having seemed to neglect them; she explained that her family and household duties had made her almost a recluse. Except for her Missionary Society and P.T.A. she never went anywhere. "You have been so good for my little girl... I want you to know what it's meant to me."

The next day Wendy asked Miss Rose if she could walk five blocks with her to her music lesson, "Mama will pick us up when it's over."

Rose wondered if she were doing the right thing to expose herself to the nostalgic days. Nobody in the town knew her past existence... she supposed that was why they felt stand-offish toward her... she seemed to be a woman of mystery. But not to Wendy! She would go. Fact was, she started looking forward to meeting her teacher and observing her method of piano instruction.

She was pleased to find she was an exponent of Edwin Hughes, of the famous Edwin Hughes' Master Classes in New York City.

On their way the little girl pointed to the oriental-looking house where 'they' said the Chinaman lived. "We must cross the street to stay away from it or something terrible will happen to us."

"No, Wendy, that's not true," and Miss Rose deliberately went up to the front door and a nice man came out to greet her. "Here is your paper, Sir, a little dog was running away with it."

He thanked her and introduced himself. But Wendy held to her convictions, "That's just *his* butler. See, it has a red clay tile roof with the corners curled up just like the ones in my geography book... and look at all those vines covering the side walls and the Chinese pagoda in the yard. He's a Mandarin all right."

When the lesson was over Mama was sitting in the car. When we got to Union Street and Alabama Avenue Wendy pointed out to Miss Rose the old hospital. "It was once used for the Confederate soldiers during the Civil War, but it's just for sick people now. If Mama would stop the car a minute we could see if Dr. Dubose is in."

"Oh, Wendy, Miss Rose doesn't care about that -- besides it's getting late."

"Please, Mama, just a second. If he's there... see that old parrot in the cage hanging on the side porch of the house next door?... well, he'll croak a few times and holler, "Dr. Dubose is operating -- puke... puke! Let me out o'here... let me out!" He hated the smell of ether.

Surely enough, Wendy was right. That old bird was setting up a howl and putting up a terrible fury in his confined area, practically banishing the good surgeon to perdition.

"My, but you have some interesting things going on in this town. How delightful your Selma is," said Rose.

"Will you come to my recital in two weeks?"

"I would love to if you have room for me."

"Did you hear, Mama, we do have room, don't we?"

From some remarks exchanged between Mrs. Pollard and Rose, Wendy felt that her neighbor next door was much more than she let on to be. So next time she saw Rose she suddenly asked her how could she form a diminished seventh chord.

"Why, Wendy, do you ask me that?"

"Because people don't go round talking about augmented sixths and dominant fifths unless..."

"Tomorrow, perhaps... I'll tell you a true story. Now I must go, dear."

Wendy's Barnabus

There was an awful lot of scale practicing going on at Wendy's house. Rose smiled and thought of the wonderful days of her own childhood, except something was missing: Wendy didn't have a pet. She wondered if her parents would object to an animal... they *did* eat a lot. Or better still, maybe she could get one and say it was for herself, but tell Wendy she was his mistress, she was just going to 'board him'.

Rose discovered that finding a St. Bernard dog was a more difficult thing than she anticipated. The local veterinarian could surely find one better than she. So it was arranged. A month later the vet gave her a call. He had a beauty -- half grown, and lovely manners. Rose fell for him at first sight. He hopped right into the taxi with her. When she got home he followed at her heels. "Oh, my boy, you're the most wonderful dog I've ever seen." When they entered the house she showed him his quarters... an old wicker chair... and his eating nook. She was told that when he needed to go out for his necessities he would indicate by putting his paw on her lap.

She couldn't wait to see Wendy's face when she confronted him. The next day they were introduced and Wendy was enthralled.

"He's all yours, dear, but I'm going to board him for you. Your mother has enough to do without a big dog around. He can go with you to your music lesson and wait on the front porch until you finish."

"Is he a St. Bernard? I've seen pictures of them in books carrying little barrels under their neck to rescue people lost in the Alps. Oh, thank you, Miss Rose. But how will he know he's mine?"

"Because you will come over at five p.m. everyday and give him his food and stroke him. I won't ever touch him. What will you call him?"

"How would St. B. do?"

Rose almost flipped -- "Why not call him 'Barnabus,'" she said. "Yes, that's perfect," agreed Wendy.

"I wouldn't tell anybody about him yet... not until your mother falls in love with him. She would not want me to be troubled with *your* dog!"

The next few months passed pleasantly. Soon it would be Spring. Rose finally had word from Bayreuth that everything was fine. Isobel was looking forward to a trip to America to see Rose in May. Rose was beside herself with joy. The lilacs would be in bloom, also the magnolias and camellias. She and Uncle Jessie started spring cleaning; he first bringing an old dog house that was abandoned so Barnabus could be outdoors more. The windows sparkled, the floors were polished, fresh flowers were in vases.

"Sho looks mightly hansome, I knows Miss Isobel will be comfortable."

"I hope you can come and help me out tomorrow; she will arrive in a cab about noon time."

"Yes, Mam, hit'l be a pleasure." The taxi drove up just at noon and the closest to a run Rose had done since the *Titanic* disaster disclosed her physical weakness. Such hugging went on that Wendy, peeking through the window curtain, felt a twinge of jealousy. And she was going to tell me a real story... now I'll have to wait!... thought the child.

On Monday Wendy had to go to school and when she got home 'that lady' was still there. "Why doesn't she leave?" Wendy said aloud. "But I'll have to face her when I go over to feed Barnabus."

Suddenly a Ford T Model drove up and the door slammed noisily. The man who was hurrying in Miss Rose's house was carrying a black satchel. She certainly couldn't go over now with all those people there.

But next door Isobel was holding Rose close as she struggled to get out the few words, "My manuscript... p.pen... write: 'Sorry, my sweet Wendy, you'll have to *read* the story I was going to tell you. But I'll see you at Carnegie Hall!'"

The doctor shook his head at Jessie and Isobel,

"Her heart; worse case I've ever seen." Rose gasped --
tried to utter something to the black man. "Take -- care
of -- my -- Wen -- d -- y ----."

After an hour or so the doctor left. It occurred to
Wendy that the visitor had got sick in the night or maybe on the ocean... then a knock sounded on her back
door. It was Uncle Jessie. "What is it?" she called out.

"Come here, chile... how can I tell you"... and his
voice choked up.

Wendy grabbed his arm, "Is it Barnabus?" Jessie's
head dropped to his chest. "No, Miss Wendy... It's Miss
Rose. Honey, she's gone... she's gone to be with her
Lord."

EPILOGUE

Carnegie Hall -- at last!

No one knew that Barnabus belonged to Wendy. The veterinarian came and got him and left the refund check with Isobel. Uncle Jessie and Isobel packed up the few things that Rose had acquired, and Jessie was to take them to remember Rose by. It was then that Isobel told the old man all about Rose and her professional career as a concert pianist who had played for the Crowned Heads of England and Europe.

"I knowed it all the time, Miss. She changed everybody's life that came to know her. God just loaned her to the world for a while."

Wendy suffered a terrible loss over the death of her old friend. As the days went by 'time' healed and left a sweetness of memories later in the little girl's life. But at first she experienced a bit of bitterness and anger... and those close to her felt its cutting edge. Through determination, though, she worked harder than ever with her music and after earning her teacher's degree, went on to study privately with Edwin Hughes in New York City.

She *did* get to Carnegie Hall... but it was with her young Civil Engineer husband. Wendy felt that she didn't really 'let Miss Rose down'; because it was through the love of music that she and Richard had met.

She closed her eyes... Miss Rose was somewhere in that vast hall. Wendy smiled to herself. "Thank you, Rose. I'll keep your memory alive through my music."

It was the year 1940.

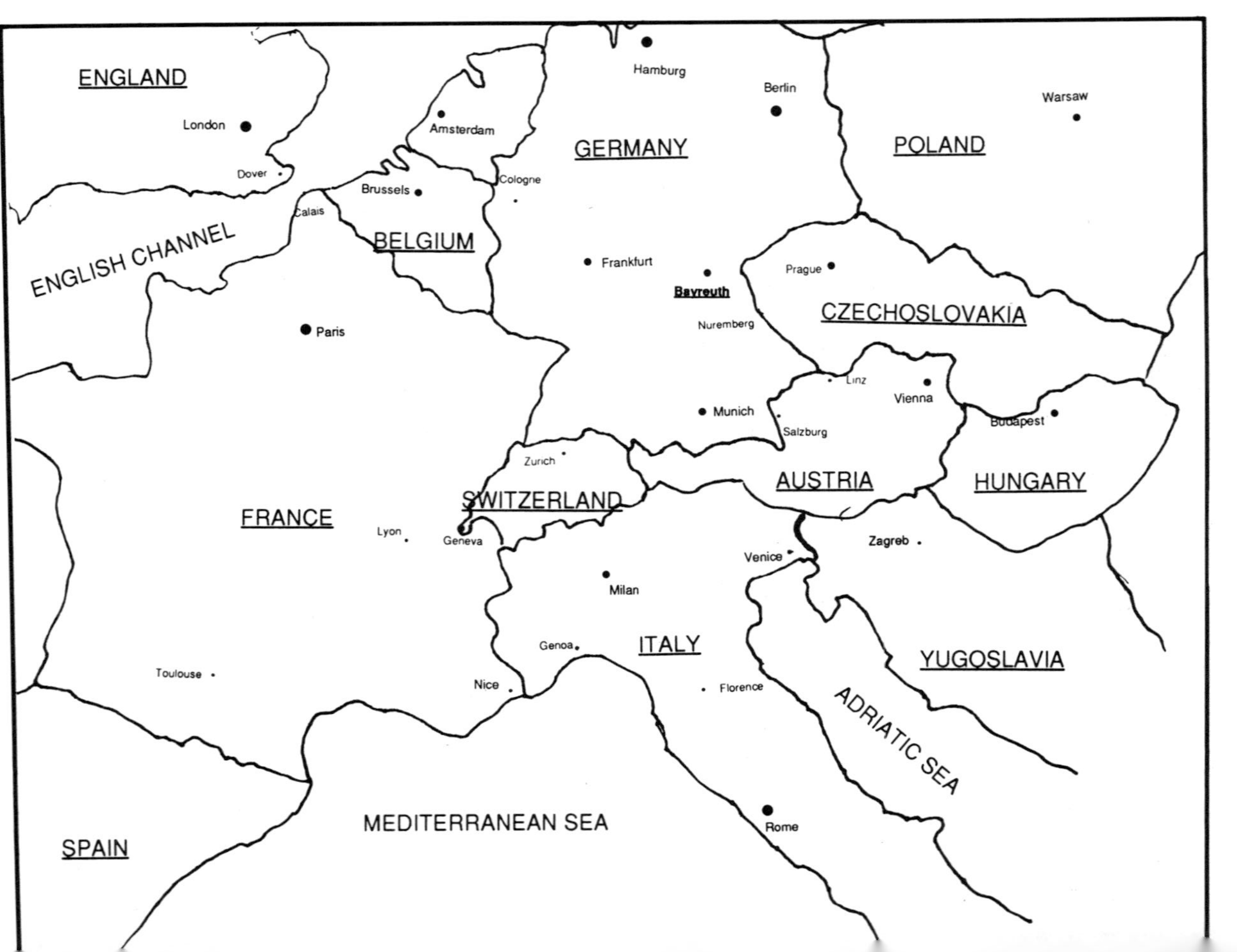

ENGLAND
London
Dover
ENGLISH CHANNEL
Hamburg
Berlin
Warsaw
GERMANY
POLAND
Amsterdam
Cologne
Brussels
Calais
BELGIUM
Frankfurt
Prague
Bayreuth
CZECHOSLOVAKIA
Nuremberg
Paris
Linz
Vienna
Munich
Salzburg
Budapest
Zurich
AUSTRIA
HUNGARY
SWITZERLAND
FRANCE
Lyon
Geneva
Zagreb
Venice
Milan
Genoa
ITALY
YUGOSLAVIA
Toulouse
Nice
Florence
ADRIATIC SEA
MEDITERRANEAN SEA
SPAIN
Rome